# SOFT SECURITY THREATS AND EUROPEAN SECURITY

This book offers an in-depth assessment of 'soft security' threats in Europe and Eurasia. These threats are now posed by many kinds of trafficking and are being responded to with a range of methods.

Experts from around the world are brought together to provide a detailed analysis of the various aspects of trafficking, covering illegal migrants, the black market weapons trade, sex trafficking and drugs. They consider the nature of this threat facing society and the effectiveness of national and international attempts to eradicate it. An assessment of EU responses to 'soft security' and a case study of US Homeland Security discuss the latest developments in this key area.

Is the concept of 'soft security' useful to analysts and policymakers? Will they be able to manage these sources of insecurity successfully in the future? This work provides likely trends and projections to resolve these pressing questions. This was first published as a special issue of *European Security*.

**Dr. Graeme P. Herd** is Professor of Civil-Military Relations, George C. Marshall European Center for Security Studies, Garmisch-Partenkirchen, Germany. He is also a Research Associate, New Security Issues Programme, Chatham House and Honorary Research Associate, Conflict Studies Research Center (CSRC), Defence Academy, UK. He has published over 80 book chapters or articles on aspects of Post-Soviet security politics.

**Anne Aldis** is Research Manager at the Conflict Studies Research Centre. For many years she has edited the Centre's publications, as well as the Strategic and Combat Studies Institute's *The Second Chechen War* and *Central and Eastern Europe: Problems and Prospects.*

# SOFT SECURITY THREATS AND EUROPEAN SECURITY

Edited by

*Anne Aldis*
*and*
*Graeme P. Herd*

Routledge
Taylor & Francis Group
LONDON AND NEW YORK

First published 2005 by Routledge
2 Park Square, Milton Park, Abingdon, Oxon OX14 4RN
52 Vanderbilt Avenue, New York, NY 10017

*Routledge is an imprint of the Taylor & Francis Group, an informa business*



Typeset in Baskerville by
Integra Software Services Pvt. Ltd, Pondicherry, India



*British Library Cataloguing in Publication Data*
A catalogue record for this book is available from the British Library

*Library of Congress Cataloging in Publication Data*
A catalog record for this book has been requested

ISBN 13: 978-0-415-37021-9 (hbk)

# CONTENTS

# THE REVOLUTION IN SECURITY AFFAIRS: HARD AND SOFT SECURITY DYNAMICS IN THE 21ST CENTURY

JULIAN LINDLEY-FRENCH

## INTRODUCTION

Uncertainty is the defining feature of the contemporary international security environment. In such an environment, what constitutes power becomes extremely complicated, particularly the role and utility of coercion. Consequently, the nature of threats, risks, and challenges and those forces that generate them require a far broader concept of security and the tools necessary to achieve desired end-states. Such uncertainty is almost certain to continue progressively revolutionizing the assumptions that drive security policy.

The old truism that linked levels of destructive power with the size and power of states is evaporating. New non-state actors have the potential, if not now then in the near future, to gain access to weapons of mass destruction and mass disruption that planners would have deemed impossible even only a few years ago. That was the essential lesson of 11 September 2001. While the "weapons" used were civilian airliners, the catastrophic nature of terrorist intent, the backgrounds of the people who carried out the attacks, and the overwhelmingly civilian targets changed the traditional concept of "the enemy." Be it transnational organised crime or catastrophic terrorism, the neat dividing lines between hard and soft, civil and military are rapidly dissolving, requiring far more flexibility on the part of Western state security institutions than has hitherto been the case. It is nothing short of a revolution in security affairs.

Thus, hard and soft security and the approaches implied therein are not just about different tools for different security problems and intensities, but, rather, what constitutes a desired security end-state in the modern world and how the West can achieve it. The result, in the West at least, has been one of confusion, as allies and partners have disagreed significantly about how to manage such complexity. Indeed, whether states in the Euro-Atlantic community emphasize hard or soft security reflects their concepts of security, the seriousness with which they take security, and the levels of investment they are prepared to put into it.

For Americans, hard security leadership is increasingly a leitmotif of overall US leadership of the West, in particular their ability to undertake "kick down the door" operations. And yet, as Iraq has demonstrated, the US remains politically resistant, and the US Army doctrinally resistant, to the complexities and commitments required for managing all parts of the security cycle, even if they are being dragged ever deeper into the mires of nation-building. Americans still do not do windows but at least they should buy a bucket.[1]

1. A lot has happened since Bush Advisor John Hillen famously rejected the role of nation-building in American security engagement during the 2000 election campaign. Clearly, a significant part of the Administration and the Pentagon still remains resistant to a role the importance of which Iraq has only served to

*(continued)*

Equally, for a lot of Europeans soft security, far from reflecting an alternative way of "doing" security to the Americans, seems to have become a metaphor for strategic pretence and free-riding by those states that would prefer to continue with the strategic vacation they have been enjoying since the end of the Cold War. Clearly, there are still too many Europeans who continue to recognize only as much threat as they can afford. For them soft security too often means no security commitment at all. That must end.

## THE TRANSATLANTIC SECURITY DILEMMA

And therein lies the transatlantic security dilemma. Whereas America needs the European allies for its excessively hard security policy to work effectively, it refuses to recognize the extent of that need because of the implications such a recognition would have for American political control over security outcomes. Until (and if) Europe's security and defense ambitions are realized in a meaningful sense (as opposed to the purely rhetorical), Europeans will continue to need Americans to inject hard security rigor into the diplomatic, aid, and development focus of their security efforts.

Unfortunately, too many Europeans seem impervious to the reality that European security without the United States will require from them a far greater level of security investment, military reorganization and political determination than they seemed prepared to make. Thus, Americans call on Europeans to do more without accepting the political price of an activist Europe, while Europeans complain about American heavy-handedness without showing any real desire to invest in the European alternative and thus increase their dependence on Americans. The result is a curious historical role reversal in which Americans talk of balances of power, strategic pre-eminence, pre-emption, and interests, whereas Europeans talk of

reinforce. As Ted Galen Carpenter put it '. . . the view articulated by Condoleezza Rice during the campaign, namely that there should be a division of labor between the European allies and the United States, with the US, focusing on serious security matters, is likely to win out in the long run.' Indeed, such a division of labor remains a Bush Administration objective. Europe sees it differently.

Woodrow Wilson-type high idealism in a tone at times reminiscent of Herbert Hoover and Senator Vandenburg-type isolationism.

In effect, the war in Iraq and its aftermath accelerated structural changes in the transatlantic relationship that were already underway. Clearly, the demands made on Europeans who were engaged (and even those who were not) uncovered weaknesses in European decision-making and capabilities that could, if not managed carefully, paralyze the EU's security tools, be they soft or hard. The pre-September 11 game in which Europeans pretended to acquire capabilities and the Americans pretended to believe them can no longer be sustained in a world in which comforting post-Cold War illusions have been shattered.

Furthermore, the split over Iraq did not simply span the Atlantic but ran through the heart of the EU and reinforced the need for some rigorous redefinitions and consensus on what is threat and what is security in Europe. Unfortunately, soft security as a concept seems to exist more in the classroom than in the field. It is profoundly unclear what specific tools soft security entails, how they would be controlled and directed and what the interface would be between soft and hard security in practice. This reinforces an impression that in fact the last thing Europeans really want is for the Americans to call their bluff and invite Europe to play a fuller role.

Such ambiguities are intrinsically linked to the problem of defining a European Union strategic concept. Although the Solana European Security Strategy presented to the European Council at Thessaloniki on 20 June 2003 was a useful first step, it was not a strategic concept that laid down a clearly agreed and understood set of principles and guidelines for the use of both co-optive and coercive European power.[2] Europeans simply do not agree on such matters.

2. Solana's paper identified three threats for Europe which have been used to redefine the so-called Petersberg Tasks that will form the missions for the forthcoming Common Security and Defence Policy (CSDP): terrorism, the proliferation of weapons of mass destruction and failed states and organized crime (which is technically four threats). Solana went on to say that the EU should be 'More active in pursuing all our strategic objectives. In particular, more active policies are needed to counter the new, dynamic threats. As a Union of 25 members, spending a total of 160 billion Euros on defence, we should, if required, be able to sustain several operations simultaneously.' See Solana J., *A Secure Europe in a Better World* (Brussels: EU, 20 June 2003) p. 13.

As such, the Solana paper was a "pre-concept" that stated what was important for Europe but did not and could not say what Europe was prepared to do about it. It might in time lead to a true European Union strategic concept, just as the EU's proposed Constitutional Treaty might one day lead to a true EU constitution that would bear some resemblance to that of a nation-state.[3]

A fundamental task of the soon to be Common Security and Defence Policy (CSDP) will be to progressively harmonize national strategic concepts so that the CSDP becomes "common" in fact, as well as in name.[4] Until then, contending strategic concepts will continue to reflect political divergence over the priorities to be given to different threats, whether they are indeed threats, and the tools, timing, and resources that will be needed to confront them. Therefore, the balance between hard and soft concepts of security is as much a European problem as it is a transatlantic problem.

That is why for Europeans the importance of Iraq has become so much more than a debate about the rights and wrongs of intervening in Iraq and removing Saddam Hussein from power. Indeed, Iraq could not have happened at a worse moment for Europe. The combination of the Iraq War, NATO and EU enlargements, shifts in the political balance of power implied therein, economic downturn, the economic and fiscal constraints of the Euro, the forthcoming European Constitution, the deadline of 2003 set in 1999 for completion of the EU's Headline Goal, and the embryonic search for a European strategic concept and method, not to mention an interventionist administration in Washington grappling with a revolutionary security situation, was surely a coincidence of events that is unlikely to be repeated. Equally, the force of those events cannot be

---

3. The choice of the title Constitutional Treaty is interesting and highlights the nature of the EU and its state of development. A constitution is normally of a state whereas a treaty is normally between states.

4. The Draft Treaty establishing a Constitution for Europe states: 'The tasks referred to in Article I-40 (1), in the course of which the Union may use civilian and military means, shall include joint disarmament operations, humanitarian and rescue tasks, military advice and assistance tasks, conflict prevention and peacekeeping tasks, tasks of combat forces in crisis management, including peacemaking and post-conflict stabilisation. All these tasks may contribute to the fight against terrorism, including supporting third countries in combating terrorism in their territories.' Article III-210 (1) of the *Draft Treaty Establishing a Constitution for Europe* (Brussels: EU 18 July 2003) p. 162.

denied. Therefore 2003 was a strategic tipping point in both Europe and the transatlantic relationship that will not be reversed. Thus, those who hope for a return to a status quo ante are living a strategic delusion. The West must cope with a new set of problems, with a new set of relationships in a new set of ways, in search of a new set of tools.

## EUROPE'S CHALLENGE

At its most stark, the post-Iraq era will force European states to make fundamental and urgent choices about how and where to invest limited resources in pursuit of complex security end-states in a post-modern, complex security environment where such choices have been avoided since the end of the Cold War. For Europeans this problem is particularly pressing, because their armed forces are those that were decided 13 years ago when threat had been banished along with the Soviet Union and the world was going to be both new and ordered. In other words, if Europe is to develop an alternative, effective, and credible way of doing security then decisions will have to be made now about the shape, structure, and cost of such an architecture.

It will take another security and defense planning cycle before such ambitions can ever become reality. Sadly, even given the epoch-changing events of the first three years of the 21st century much of the rhetoric associated with European "defense" seems more a continued avoidance of hard choices than a determination to confront them; part of an emerging Emperor's New Clothes approach to security that will afford little or no real security in an increasingly dangerous world. It is a depressing but compelling thought that new combinations are emerging in which global imbalances in wealth and power and the spread of catastrophic weapons technology (much of which is now over 60 years old) fuels the emergence of catastrophically armed fundamentalism. It is not an exaggeration to suggest that if the 21st century continues along the path upon which it seems to have embarked, it will be at least as violent as the 20th and possibly more so. This is no time for Europe to be obsessed with process instead of substance.

Thus, there are certain security truisms that Europeans must confront. First, no single European state can afford or affect the security environment. Intense cooperation between Europeans is a sine qua non for the adequate protection of the European citizen and that means a strong European Union. Second, there is clearly a European interest in security effectiveness that can only be afforded by far closer security cooperation.

Third, the very nature of soft security concepts places a premium upon legitimate action that can only be afforded through the imprimatur of legitimacy that transnational political and military institutions such as NATO and the EU generate. The European Union will in all probability become the focal point of Europe's security and defence in the future, with NATO retaining its vital role as the transatlantic interoperability nexus and platform for global power projection. However, if the EU aspires to such a role then it must be based upon true security policy coherence and real security tools, and be backed up by a credible military capability that bears some relation to the environment in which it exists. What Europe does not need is a false European security policy under the banner of the Common Foreign and Security Policy (CFSP), which, while rhetorically powerful, is in fact a means of avoiding the burdens of security. That would leave Europe in the worst of all worlds, with an EU that lacks security and defense credibility, and a NATO that is politically paralyzed in a Europe replete with contending strategic concepts, none of which are properly tooled for the challenges that inevitably lie ahead.

In that context, the Iraq War represents the final and irrevocable breakdown of the Cold War order and the Cold War transatlantic relationship and the stripping back of institutional pretense to reveal new forms of informal multilateral groupings that will form and dissolve around issues and events. The future is inevitably one in which the very political nature of strategic collective security will see political coalitions of the willing and able that often bring together partners with significantly different views about how to manage complex security. Both Europeans and Americans will find themselves with less security structure at a time when they need to create more security effect.

## AMERICA'S CHALLENGE

Even an informal partnership will present challenges for the United States. The Bush Administration seems driven by a belief that exceptional American power makes America exceptionally vulnerable, and thus confers upon the US an exceptional right to act beyond multilateral frameworks with an almost universal application of hard power. In exceptional circumstances, such as the Global War on Terror (the direct war, not the inferred war that took place in Iraq), that position was both justifiable and sustainable. However, it would be a mistake of significant political proportions for the US to believe that the Global War on Terror represented a kind of political blank check for attacking states of concern or removing regimes that fail to live up to America's standards. One of the tragedies of Iraq is that it took place just as the natural political momentum of 11 September 2001 was slowing and the search for a new "grand strategy" between America and its partners was underway. It should be clearly understood that virtually no Europeans supported the US over Iraq and the majority of those who did seem to have done so either out of loyalty to American leadership or as a result of the disciplining ability of American power.

The abandonment of any attempt to assess the intent of a state and to judge a threat purely on the basis of perceived capabilities, volatile rhetoric, or indirect links to indistinct groups has created a situation in which America's "right" of action has been dangerously de-legitimized. In effect, American actions of late have not so much suggested unilateralism but rather is assertive isolationism.

Indeed, such a rejection of that tradition would be proof to the world that the inspirational American idea in international relations was at an end. In such a complex security environment right is essential to successful governance. As Iraq has demonstrated, contemporary security is inherently political, almost more so than in the past, when the fact of weak states and 24/7 TV coverage make the relationship between state power and the individual, both ally and adversary alike, far more intimate. Iraq has also demonstrated not just the awesome power of America but the limits of that power, because it is striking both how little of America's available power the politics of the conflict have permitted and how the majority of the jobs that modern military machines have to do are not those they are trained for. In the final analysis, modern conflict is an armored party political broadcast.

America created modern international law. It is in America's interests to live by it, because ultimately it is inspirational America that will make the world a better place, not just mighty America, and as *the* status quo power America needs the system to work for it. Certainly, no actor can consider security without considering it at its broadest. Not to do so, to opt out of any part of the full cycle from conflict prevention through to post-conflict re-construction, is to leave security policy dangerously unbalanced. It is striking that balance and agreeing upon it that is the essential political dilemma for and between Europeans and Americans and which underpins the political debate over hard and soft security.

## IN SEARCH OF A TRANSATLANTIC STRATEGIC CONCEPT

Concepts of security on the two sides of the Atlantic have changed radically over the past 2 years as a result of the attacks on the US of 11 September 2001 and the Second (or third) Gulf War. Nor is it just a transatlantic phenomenon, because Europe is also self-evidently split asunder. North Americans and Europeans are now split into three, maybe four, camps, reflecting these contending security concepts. One camp is led by those in the United States who argue that while in the past one may have had the time and the reasonable certainty to examine both intent and capabilities when assessing threat, the reality post-September 11 has revealed a terrible new specter posed by the possible fusion of non-state actors, weak states, and weapons of mass destruction into a form of strategic asymmetry that has the power to expose the weaknesses of even the most powerful.

Given that perception, the US seems to believes it no longer prudent to wait to assess intention but, rather, it must on occasion strike pre-emptively to assure its security because its very power and status makes it far more vulnerable than others. It is to some a reinterpretation of Articles 7 and 51 of the UN Charter, while to others reflective of a demand that the UN and its instruments be modernized to cope with a reality for which it is simply not prepared, otherwise the UN will lose all relevance to the special security needs of the US.

Another group that has come to coalesce around the French position, reflecting perhaps a lessened sense of threat, reflective also, perhaps, of a lessened sense of power, appears to be arguing that *no*: intent still matters and must be assessed far more carefully than hitherto before any call to arms can be made. Not least because of the nature of that new threat which can never be defeated by decisive military action alone. This is the case even if a linkage between weak states, catastrophic terror, and, indeed, global reach organised crime were proven. For this group the role of the UN remains pivotal, because the political aspects of security governance demand balance between power and the legitimacy afforded by the UN. Consequently, even if a regime is, in the words of Resolution 1441, technically in "material breach," automaticity of action does not follow. Moreover, past UN resolutions cannot provide a cumulative audit trail justifying action because contexts, intents and, indeed, capabilities change. This requires a constant process of engagement and re-evaluation of what soft and hard tools to apply and the balance between cooption and coercion.

There is a third group, several of whom can also be found in Europe, loosely grouped around Germany, who seem to be rejecting all forms of coercive diplomacy and, indeed, coercion in international relations. It is a perfectly respectable viewpoint that is founded upon a well-elaborated tradition that was first championed in the Palais des Nations in Geneva in the aftermath of the First World War and which still infuses to a significant extent the foreign and security policies of many European countries and not a few others.

Then there is a fourth group, which is made up of members of at least two of the other groups, effective of their friends. First, whereas Europeans' security has been guaranteed for the past 60 years by being close to the US, they now suspect it is best served by maintaining a distance. This group often talks through the metaphors of hard and soft security, using it as code to object to America's strategic concept, that is, its use of coercion. Second, Europeans should seek an alternative road to security governance.

However, while old Europe/new Europe is a bit strong (one would hardly include Britain in new Europe however attractive that might appear to New Labor as it tries to squeeze the last drop of political capital out of "cool Britannia"), fractured Europe is a reality. Indeed, Europe is faced with a fundamental strategic choice: either get real about the continuing role of justifiable coercion in international relations and build structures accordingly that can act as transmission points between a European concept of hard and soft security. Or, accept that Europe's concept of security is a sham and that the United States will decide by right and might when and how to apply power in whatever soft/hard combination it chooses.

This strategic choice has been made all the more stark by the harsh confrontation between America and France in the United Nations Security Council prior to the attack on Iraq. Again, Iraq was not really about Iraq but rather about the nature, the role, the balance, and the authorization of coercion in global security governance by the dominant grouping, and its relationship with co-option, in the face of many threats now being generated by non-traditional actors in non-traditional ways.

On the American side, their changing perceptions of threat in the wake of 11 September and the role that allies can play in American security and defense, have led to a downgrading of the value of allies as security partners, especially for this administration.[5] For the Bush administration, the shocking and violent nature of September 11 has also led to a downsizing of soft security as an integral part of ongoing security management and the championing of harder, more immediate, more visible military aspects. The result? The acceleration of a tendency that was all too apparent before Iraq and which came to a head in those stark confrontations in the UN Security Council. An America that now tends to over-militarize security, and a Europe that tends to over-civilianize it. It is this marked difference in transatlantic strategic concepts has split the *organization* of Europe's security and defense into two further camps.

The first, led by the French, suggest that Europe can no longer afford to follow the United States for political, security, military-technical, or even financial reasons and that Europe should really move from the ambition to construct an autonomous security and defense structure to one that is genuinely independent. Unfortunately, the gap between Europe's vital interests and its ability to do anything about it is so large that it will be a long time before Europe's softer approach to security can ever be underpinned by credible military power. Kofi Annan has pointed out the danger of offering diplomatic carrots without a credible military stick.

The other camp, naturally led by the British, rejects this revisionist view of transatlantic relations, arguing strongly that European security, particularly extra-European interests, can only be safeguarded by remaining close to the world's only historical example of hyper-power.

5. Although this assessment of the value of allies and partners might be changing in light of the limits of American power being demonstrated by Iraq.

Ironically, this camp harbors as many of the same concerns about some of the people floating around the margins of the Bush administration as the first camp, but it accepts Tony Blair's argument that it is better to be on the inside battling therein than on the outside attacking from without. Either approach, as the British, French and Germans have found to their costs, carries political dangers. However, implicit in all their approaches is the same objective—influencing America.

## HARD AMERICA, SOFT EUROPE

That said, the European security agenda and the American security agenda do reflect different security emphases. Europe's obsessions are not those of America. Illegal migration, the trafficking of people and drugs, and the power of organized crime and weapons transfers all touch on homeland security in the broadest sense but lack the compelling immediacy of catastrophic terrorism. Soft threats are the stuff of much of Europe's security today, not the traditional conflict between uncertain states in an uncertain international environment, but, rather, between uncertain states dealing with determined and purposeful non-state actors. Actors that often emerge from weak or failing states with the capacity to generate the power to exploit the open interconnectivity that is a hallmark of Western societies in a way that can make even the most powerful vulnerable.

The policy dilemma for the West is that it tends to exacerbate threats by overly compartmentalizing responses for the sake of national, bureaucratic, and policy tidiness. That is a mistake. There are very reasonable grounds to believe that a threat continuum exists between transnational organized crime, catastrophic terror, and corrupt regimes in some weak states. Any response therefore requires holistic, strategic, and pan-national civil-military responses working within states and between states, often with a global reach. Not only does the required flexibility not come easily to the bureaucratic mind but the military and civil approaches to security, particularly policing, are founded on very different principles and methods, making such an organizational and effects-based response continuum difficult to realize in practice. However, even the briefest of analyses of organized crime and catastrophic terror underlines the scale of this challenge and the self-defeating nature of the political imbroglio that has paralyzed the West and from which its enemies have drawn real succour.

The war will not be won easily. Indeed, the nature and sophistication of the enemy is sobering, as the 10 points below demonstrate:

1. They can generate threat anywhere and rapidly;
2. They are often part of Western societies as well as enemies of it and thus can achieve tactical supremacy, even battlespace dominance at a point and time of their choosing. That was a vital lesson of 11 September;
3. They have highly redundant systems which can take a great deal of damage and still operate;
4. They can penetrate to the heart of decision-making structures, particularly those of weaker states that by definition are important partners in the global war on terror;
5. They are constantly reconnoitering weak points to attack. The West offers a multitude of targets, particularly critical national infrastructure;[6]
6. They draw no moral distinction between civilian and military targets. Indeed, civilian targets seem preferable as part of their Information Warfare and Psyops strategy. They certainly do not play by any clearly defined set of rules;
7. They will use any level of destructive power they can get their hands on. They seek not to negotiate, but simply to generate spectacular effect;

6. The degree of vulnerability of Western societies and the complexity of dealing with attacks is apparent in a recent IISS Adelphi Paper which states, '. . . attackers can be of two types. They may be non-state actors whose purposes are criminal and who are subject to the jurisdiction of one or more sovereign states. Their attacks constitute crimes against individuals and property. Terrorists constitute a more serious set of non-state actors and are of concern both to law enforcement agencies and national security agencies. The second type of attacker is a sovereign state waging information warfare. The attacker's targets are other sovereign states, although specific targets may be identical to those of non-state attackers. Defence against these attackers is a responsibility of both external and internal security and intelligence agencies, acting in concert.' See Lukasik, Stephen J., Goodman, Seymour E. and Longhurst, David W. *Protecting Critical Infrastructures Against Cyber-Attack*, Adelphi Paper 359, (Oxford: OUP 2003) p. 11.

8. They communicate as much implicitly as explicitly, which makes penetration of what is a flat and loose cellular hierarchy very difficult;
9. They can reconstitute rapidly and withstand critical losses, and generate massive destructive and disruptive power at minimal cost, exacting such high ratio strategic leverage that some traditional allies are quietly considering whether their security is best served by being part of the Global War on Terror or by maintaining a distance from it.
10. They draw their support from a large pool of fellow travellers whose hearts and minds will take a very long time to change.

Thus, catastrophic terror creates a form of strategic asymmetry that keeps traditional states off-balance and poses a profound intellectual dilemma for political leaders, defense planners, police chiefs, and civil authorities, all schooled in the rigors of symmetry and well-defined roles. The enemy strikes in the strategic gap between excessive American heaviness and excessive European lightness, between America's strategic concept and Europe's want of one, and between civil and military concepts of security. Consequently, they exacerbate, even generate, the emerging divide in the strategic concepts not only on both sides of the Atlantic but between Europeans. This spills over into policy choices Europeans are making about how and whether to confront the security challenges. A dilemma highlighted by Javier Solana's paper on a European Security Strategy.

## THE REVOLUTION IN SECURITY AFFAIRS

To conclude, flexibility, consistency, and patience will be vital in the emerging hard/soft security environment. However, without new thinking about the nature of the threats and the structure of the West's response to it, security could fail. Catastrophic terrorism will never destroy the West but the damage to it, together with the loss of confidence in business and even the coherence of society, would entail such a change to the Western way of life that terror would have been deemed to have won. That must not happen.

Given the challenges the West faces, agreement between Americans and Europeans on a new balance between cooption and coercion is a matter of some urgency. A new transatlantic security covenant is needed at a strategic level to reaffirm the commitment to each other and to the mission. There will need to be a transatlantic concept of pre-emption. A range of practical lower-level initiatives will be equally important. Macro-security will not work in such an environment unless it is supported by effective effects-based micro-security.

Increased transnational co-operation between agencies and structures will be essential. Military and criminal intelligence will need to work far more closely together. There needs to be a much more effective interface between military and civil tools of security. This will be particularly important in post-conflict societies, such as Afghanistan and Iraq, where civil society institutions need to be reconstructed. Combat forces need to be released from peacekeeping, possibly through the increased use of paramilitary forces, such as Italy's Carabinieri and Spain's Guardia Civile. In the longer run, the roles of international governmental and non-governmental organizations need to be reinforced, primarily in reducing the pools of despair and hopelessness that fuel such threats, and a lot more money pumped through. Security investment for security effect will be the key phrase of the age. Such an approach will include better and more effective distribution of aid, and the reconstruction of civil societies and their institutions devastated by poverty and poor governance. The rich West must invest in the poor South not out of largesse but as a practical recognition of its own interests.

Finally, concepts of what is security and how it can be achieved will need to be constantly reassessed in a constantly changing security environment in which the old certainties are fast evaporating. We need to be clear about what it is we want to achieve and to know when we have achieved it. Events of late demonstrate the urgency of the policy choices that the West must confront as the West. In that context soft security must mean real security and not a convenient slogan for avoiding the hard responsibilities of security. The enemy makes no distinction between soft Europe and hard America. What is needed is nothing less than a revolution in security affairs.

# ILLEGAL MIGRATION: UKRAINE

LEONID POLYAKOV

Soon after becoming an independent country in 1991, Ukraine found itself strongly concerned about all forms of migration, including illegal migration. Military conflicts in neighboring countries; economic insecurity inside Ukraine itself; its specific geographical position between the West and the East (and the West and the South); and the open borders with the former Soviet republics of Russia, Belarus, and Moldova, which Ukraine inherited after the collapse of the Soviet Union—all created strong currents of migration through and out of the country.

The post-Cold War "security vacuum," and Ukraine's weak democracy, poor governance, and myriad other factors made it difficult to quickly organize an effective and efficient response. Though public and authorities' attention started to be drawn to the problem by alarming estimates and comments on the dangers posed by illegal migration as early as the mid-1990s, it took another 5–6 years for Ukraine to build, by 2003, more or less viable legal and organizational systems of managing illegal migration. These are still in need of substantial improvement, however.

The illegal migration phenomenon in all its major forms poses a significant challenge for Ukraine—it drains the human and financial resources of the state, contributes to a high level of criminality and corruption, and negatively impacts the international image of the country.

Currently, in terms of illegal migration, Ukraine is considered primarily a transit and donor country. Tens of thousands of migrants from Asia and Africa try to cross Ukraine illegally every year on their way to their dream—peaceful and prosperous Western Europe. Even greater numbers of Ukrainians attempt to find their fortunes there by leaving the country in search of work, often without having a legal arrangement; in other words, illegally. At the same time, there are visible indicators that Ukraine will soon become a desired destination country for illegal migrants too—the internal political situation is relatively stable, the climate is moderate, the economy is improving, and prospects for economic growth are encouraging.

In the European security context the illegal migration challenge for Ukraine will be an illustrative case study both in terms of its general impact on regional stability, and its experience responding to the challenge, including its national and international aspects. But to effectively respond to (in other words, manage) any security challenge one has to be able to correctly assess the situation, which includes timely measuring of the problem. This article examines the latest developments in the illegal migration situation in Ukraine, as well as national and international measures to respond to this challenge and prospects for the solution of this problem in the future.

## ILLEGAL TRANSIT MIGRATION THROUGH UKRAINE

The number of illegal migrants transiting through Ukraine and detained by Ukrainian border guards, according to official statistics, grew steadily in the 1990s from a mere 148 in 1991, to 11,444 in 1994, and to a peak of 14,646 in 1999. Then this official figure diminished threefold and stabilized at around 5000 per year in 2000–2002, while in 2003 the number of illegal migrants intercepted is likely to grow again. However, according to the head of the State Committee on Nationalities and Migration and General of militia (Ukraine's police) Gennadiy Moskal, no more than 10% of the total number of illegal migrants crossing Ukraine are being apprehended.[1] If so, then the total estimated numbers attempting to transit through Ukraine could well be at least 50,000 per year.

And, of course, not only border guards detain illegal migrants in Ukraine; other law-enforcement structures like police of the Ministry of Internal Affairs and operatives of the Security Service of Ukraine detain them as well. According to the Minister of Internal Affairs of Ukraine, General Yuriy Smirnov, for example, in 2001 alone, 28,000 migrants illegally crossed the border of Ukraine and then settled in the country without a legal permit.[2] In addition to those detained on the border by the border guards, this would make over 35,000 illegal migrants per year, which looks a more or less realistic figure.

In reality, however, this total could well be even higher, if it is true that the majority of illegal migrants are actually coming to Ukraine for allegedly legal reasons, but then violate their status and become illegal migrants, as claimed by the former head of Ukraine's Interpol branch.[3] That at the end of the decade the number of migrants detained by border guards suddenly dropped almost threefold, probably reflects the fact that some improvements in Ukraine's border regime, first of all with Russia, made potential migrants look for ways of crossing the border legally, rather than relying on human smugglers. As of late, Ukrainian authorities have recognized a significant growth in cases involving forged or illegally obtained passports

1. Orest Sokhar, 'Policemen and illegal migrants—two key problems of the country', *Polityka i Kultura*, 15–21 March 2003.

2. Ukraina.ru, 15 March 2002. 'Ukraine faces tough issue of illegal migration, admitted the head of Interior Ministry', http://www.ukraine.ru/news/121018.html.

3. Iryna Ralemska, 'Interpol counters migration (Interview with the Head of Ukraine's Interpol Victor Radetsky)', *Uriadovy Kuryer*, 18 January 2001.

of such CIS countries as Kirgizstan, Tajikistan, Georgia, Kazakhstan, Armenia, and the Russian Federation.[4] One more reason for this radical drop in the number of detentions could be the tendency not to account for those detained on the Ukraine-Russian border, but to simply send them back to Russia, or to turn the detainees over to Russian authorities. Thus the statistic of captured illegal migrants mostly reflects those who have already penetrated deep into Ukrainian territory and those captured on Ukraine's western border.[5]

The national composition of illegal migrants is subject to certain changes too. In the 1990s most migrants were coming to Ukraine from Afghanistan, Bangladesh, India, Iran, Iraq, Nigeria, Pakistan, Sri Lanka, Yemen, and other overpopulated or underdeveloped countries. However, in recent years the largest number of illegal migrants detained in Ukraine appeared to be Chinese. For instance, in the first half of 2003 the number of detained illegal migrants from China increased almost three times compared with the same period of 2002. The reasons for this phenomenon are not immediately clear, even to the experts. At the same time, some growth in the number of migrants to and through Ukraine from the Caucasus (including Chechens) has also been noticed. This is naturally linked to the unresolved ethnic and separatist conflicts in that region.

Besides illegally crossing the border and covertly travelling on Ukrainian railways and roads to the West, one of the other most commonly used channels of transferring illegal migrants through Ukraine in the recent past was to apply for education in the country's colleges and universities with the aim of sneaking to the West at the first opportunity. Such "foreign students," after arriving in Ukraine, usually cared only about arriving at the place of study and registering there. They would then quickly disappear to unknown destinations. Sometimes they would disappear without even registering.

Ukrainian authorities, after recognizing the extent of this phenomenon, have introduced several protective measures: the consular services of Ukrainian embassies in countries of concern introduced stricter procedures for issuing student visas; educational institutions now require that foreigners pay the yearly cost of tuition in advance

4. Olexandr Khomra, 'Illegal Transit Migration as a Threat to the National Security of Ukraine', *Strategichna Panorama*, No. 1, 2003, pp. 107–117.
5. Ibid.

and have introduced tighter control of their foreign students; and border service officials now conduct intensive interviewing of this category of foreign guests. Such measures brought visible results: in 2002 Ukrainian embassies' consular sections refused to issue Ukrainian entry visas to thousands of applicants for education; the same year over 1500 "foreign students" failed the interview at the border crossing point and were not allowed to enter and study in Ukraine.[6]

However, the overall numbers of illegal migrants detained by Ukraine's western neighbor countries—Poland, Slovakia, and Hungary—remain rather stable. It is very likely that this lack of visible progress is the result of the high adaptability of already mature international criminal networks aiding the transit of illegal migrants through Ukraine. According to the country's Security Service, their experience of fighting the channels of illegal trafficking proves that the criminal world has already become effective at falsifying documents, has introduced sophisticated methods of collecting, transporting, and hiding small and large groups of illegal migrants, and has established connections with corrupt officials. The number of detained foreigners and locals among criminal traffickers is roughly equal, and the criminal structures are highly secretive, well equipped, and work in parallel fashion without trying to monopolize the market.[7]

The price list for criminal services for illegal migrants is already known: a forged passport of a Western European country costs up to $1,000; crossing Ukraine's western border in a bus hideout, around $500; crossing the border through channels outside of border checkpoints, $500–$1,000; one day's stay at a private apartment, around $50. In total, the cost of illegal transit through Ukraine for one migrant could be in the range of $5,000–$6,000, which means that criminal incomes from transit of illegal migrants could total over $50 million per year.

It is not just criminal traffickers who pose an immediate threat to Ukraine's security. Illegal migrants themselves are often either common criminals, or poor uneducated individuals engaged in

6. Olga Perekhrest, 'Interview with the Head of the State Border Committee General Colonel Mykola Lytvyn: migration processes in our country could be completely under control, on the condition that there is a comprehensive approach', *Prykordonnyk Ukrainy*, 11 January 2003.

7. See: Lada Safronova, 'The window to Europe', *Novyi Vek*, 26 January 2002.

criminal business to pay for their everyday needs. Thus migration-related crime in Ukraine is often linked to other soft security threats—related activities like illegal drug and arms trafficking. There are estimates that over 70% of illegal transit migrants are carrying drugs with them. According to other estimates, in recent years in Ukraine around 40,000–50,000 migrants have become subject to administrative punishments each year (down from over 100,000 in the 1990s); some of them go to prison, while hundreds of Ukrainian local officials are facing corruption charges in cases related to illegal migration.

Naturally, the Ukrainian state tries to manage the challenge of illegal migration. In the new Criminal Code of Ukraine adopted in 1991, relevant provisions are included for the punishment of those guilty of illegal migrant trafficking. Borders with Russia, Moldova, and Belarus have been strengthened in recent years by deploying and equipping additional border guards; in 2002 the decision to increase the total number of border troops by 5000 (from their total strength of 45,000) was adopted by the Verkhovna Rada (Ukrainian Parliament), and the number of border guard units on Ukraine's eastern border with Russia almost reached the density of Ukraine's western border. Similar measures are envisioned in relation to the borders with Belarus and Moldova.

While restrictive measures against illegal migrants are on the rise, however, at the same time the country has started paying more attention to the human needs of those who fail to cross Ukraine and are detained by the authorities, steps are being taken to improve the conditions at sites of temporary detention of illegal migrants, as well as to attract more attention to them from the embassies of their home countries in Ukraine.

The continuing problematic situation with regard to illegal migrant transit through Ukraine is forcing authorities towards more resolute responsive measures: improving the legislative base, strengthening border cooperation with neighboring countries, and improving the organizational structures of responsible state institutions and their coordination. There have been certain achievements along these lines, like the adoption in 2001 of the new law on immigration and the approval by presidential decree of the "Programme for Fighting Illegal Migration for 2001–2004."

Cooperation with neighboring countries is becoming more active. For instance, in addition to traditional consultations and meetings, Ukraine has sent police liaison officers to six neighboring countries, and the officers are responsible for coordination of illegal migration issues as well. At the moment, one of the most urgent issues is probably the proper division of authority and coordination between eight executive agencies dealing with illegal migrants. In accordance with the Presidential Decree, the Cabinet of Ministers of Ukraine should have submitted a substantiated proposal on the creation of a top coordinating body called the State Migration Service to the President by the middle of 2003. However, it is still an open issue whether this service will be an independent structure, or subordinate to the Ministry of Internal Affairs, as was done in Russia.

Most importantly, Ukraine still lacks financial resources and effective international cooperative arrangements to properly organize the apprehension, prosecution, and deportation of illegal migrants. But even if the country were more prosperous and had a perfect legal base, there would be no guarantee that the situation would improve without effective multilateral efforts. It is noteworthy that some 70–80% of those who try to penetrate Ukraine illegally are coming through the border with Russia (20–25% of illegal migrants enter Ukraine from Belarus), while around 60% of those who try to leave Ukraine illegally to the West are detained at the border with Slovakia (around 20% at the Polish border).[8] However, Russia and Belarus are not very eager to sign an agreement on readmission with Ukraine, though they usually agree to accept immediately those detained on their border with Ukraine.

The positive thing is that Ukraine is not fighting the threat of illegal migration alone. The country receives some financial and technical support for "border management" from the EU (2001 - €6.75

8. Hanna Lukanska, 'Violators of vitrual borders are not prosecuted,' interview with Deputy Chief of Main Staff of the State Border Committee of Ukraine, Major-General Borys Marchenko, *Prikordonnyk Ukrainy*, 19 April 2003. 'According to the estimates of the State Border Committee (Author's note: now the Administration of State Border Service of Ukraine) around 72% of all illegal migrants are coming to our country transiting from Russia. A quarter, from the territory of Belarus.' Other, unofficial estimates put the number coming from Russia as high as 80%. In October 2003 the EU promised Ukraine 8 million euros specifically aimed at strengthening Ukraine's border with Russia and Belarus. *Korrespondent.net*, 7 October 2003.

million; 2002 - €15 million; 2003 - €7 million under the TACIS programme)[9] as well as from individual countries—first of all from the USA (through USAID, training programs, and technical support programs)—as well as from Great Britain, Germany, and others. But this is a rather small amount compared with what is needed for the country, and what the EU is providing for Ukraine's neighbors to the west—Poland, Slovakia and Hungary. For the latter, the EU spends hundreds of thousands of Euros to help establish an "impenetrable" border regime.[10]

This disparity is a concern for Ukrainian officials, as well as for the International Organisation for Migration (IOM), which advocates stronger foreign support for Ukraine and for Russia, which supplies the bulk of illegal migrants coming to Ukraine. The Ukrainian border with the enlarged EU will soon stretch for over 1400 kilometers, and Ukraine alone will not be able to effectively stop the flow of illegal migrants, who are willing to risk their lives to enter the prosperous West from the poor, deprived, and overpopulated countries of the South and East.

Even with the help currently provided to it, Ukraine still will not be able to provide for effective interception, and civilized detention and deportation of all illegal transit migrants who attempt to use its territory as a springboard for entering the EU. If support for Ukraine is not substantially increased, it is very likely that those illegal migrants who have already managed to enter Ukraine will sooner or later manage to enter the EU, despite the Union's best efforts to preclude such an outcome. If this concern is not addressed

9. Oleksiy Rozhkov, 'EU support programme to strengthen Ukraine's borders'. *Immediate Neighbourhood of Ukraine and EU*, (Uzhgorod, Valeriy Padiak Publishers 2002) p. 145.

10. See, for instance, on new equipment for Hungarian border guards: Keith Richburg, 'Security Curtain Raised Along EU's New Eastern Front: Tightened Borders Draw Concerns About Impact on Neighboring Nations', *Washington Post* Foreign Service, 31 July 2003, p. A13. '. . . new equipment to outfit the guards. There are now hand-held heat-sensing cameras that can detect a person at night a mile away, and, out in forests near the border, underground sensors that can detect anything from a heavy vehicle to a person trying to slip through. . . . The radar-equipped patrol boat is also new. . . . There is a machine that scans the inside of trucks and senses body heat. Vehicles crossing the bridge now pass between two six-foot-high cream-colored poles with radiation sensors mounted on top. . . . '

in a timely and effective fashion, the tension on the border between Ukraine and the enlarged EU may increase.

## ASPECTS OF SETTLEMENT OF ILLEGAL MIGRANTS IN UKRAINE

Already, different estimates suggest that on the territory of Ukraine there are from 500,000 to 1 million migrants, including illegal ones, who are either permanently settled in Ukraine or simply waiting for the chance to move further west. At the same time, the official estimate gives the number of registered foreign citizens in Ukraine as 250,000, of which 168,000 are considered to be permanent residents.[11] However, acquiring realistic official statistics on the number of illegal migrants settled in Ukraine is problematic at best, simply because they naturally avoid contact with the authorities.

According to Mykola Yerukh, the Head of the Refugee and Migration Directorate at the State Committee on Nationalities and Migration, the number of illegal "settlers" in Ukraine is about 10% of the total number of migrants. He suggests that this category could equal 30,000.[12] But it is very likely that the real number is much higher. For instance, according to official data, some 8177 foreigners recently arrived in Ukraine with a 3-month visa, but only 5007 left the country in time. The remaining 3170 (39%) formally became illegal migrants. In the latter group, there are 1335 citizens of Turkey, 371 from China, 265 from Iran, 235 from Syria, 204 from Lebanon, and 104 from India. They crossed the border with the declared purposes of tourism (21%), business (18%), education (12%), and transit (9%).[13] While the detailed statistical composition of this group generally reflects traditional tendencies in national representation of illegal migrants to Ukraine, it also demonstrates some new developments, since the largest group of this type of violators was from Turkey.

11. Andrey Smirnov, 'The Window to Europe', *Korrespondent,* 3 June 2003.
12. Ibid.
13. Sergey Astakhov, 'Who needs illegal migrants?' *Newspaper '2000'*, 16 May 2003.

To settle detained illegal migrants and asylum seekers, Ukrainian authorities have organized several camps in different regions of Ukraine. Due to the inadequate financing and limited space, living conditions in these camps are rather modest, if not downright poor. Especially problematic situations are observed in summer, when detention camps are overcrowded and migrants have to live there for months while waiting to be deported or otherwise dealt with. For instance, the camp "Pavshyno," located in the Trans-Carpathian region of Ukraine, is supposed to house up to 280 persons, but in summer their number could be as high as 600.[14] It is not rare in such situations that detainees revolt, harassing the security guards, breaking windows, furniture, and so on. In 2002, that happened four times.

A certain number of detained illegal migrants are not just waiting for the moment of their deportation, but also actively applying for refugee status. It is noteworthy that in January 2003, Ukraine acceded to the 1951 United Nations Refugee Convention and its 1967 Protocol. As a result, the number of registered refugee applications from illegal migrants has significantly increased. For example, in the far western Ukrainian city of Uzhgorod, the administrative centre of the Trans-Carpathian region bordering Poland, Slovakia, and Hungary, for the first half of 2003 over 500 applications for refugee status were submitted, while for all of 2002 only 70 such applications were registered.[15] It is very likely that many applicants are hoping to use the procedure and refugee status simply in order to wait in Ukraine until the moment when country's western border becomes the border with the EU, and then to try to cross the border again.

To handle thousands of cases of illegal migrants and refugee applicants who are settled or detained in Ukraine, the law-enforcement and migration authorities have very scarce budgets. International organizations like the UN, OSCE, EU, Red Cross, and IOM, as well as individual countries like the US, Germany, Austria, and others provide a degree of support, but the amount is not sufficient to make

14. Hanna Lukanska, 'Violators of virtual borders are not prosecuted: Interview with Deputy Chief of Main Staff of the State Border Committee of Ukraine General Major Borys Marchenko', *Prykordonnyk Ukrainy*, 19 April 2003.

15. Korrespondent.Net, 14 July 2003. ' For six months in Trans-Carpathian Region over 500 foreigners applied for refuge, . . . '

a noticeable difference. Still, Ukrainian experts see the primary solution for deportation of illegal migrants not only in greater amounts of foreign financial support for Ukraine, but also in the conclusion of a comprehensive system of readmission agreements. Negotiations on readmission with the EU are underway, but Ukrainian law-enforcement authorities are unenthusiastic, since they consider concluding such agreements with Russia and Belarus to be of much higher priority, and they want these agreements to be signed before the agreement with the EU. However, the first draft agreement between Ukraine and Russia on receiving and transferring of persons was developed as far back as in 1996, though Russia still considers it to be a "painful issue"[16] and signing is indefinitely delayed.

Today, only a short time after independence, migrants on the territory of Ukraine already form influential ethnic communities. Ukrainian law-enforcement authorities often ask them to take care of their nationals, but such requests are not always successful. Therefore, when neither their native embassy nor their ethnic community are willing to give them money for a ticket home, even illegal migrants often end up receiving a temporary residence permit to allow them to earn the money on their own. They are naturally in no hurry to return home from Ukraine, where they can enjoy low prices for basic consumer goods and utilities, good opportunities to work in the shadow economy, and other benefits. This situation logically leads to an accumulation of illegal migrants, and to a number of negative consequences for Ukraine.

Typically, these include bringing to the country unknown diseases and exotic religions and customs, or trying to earn quick money through criminal business like trading drugs or contraband. Illegal migrants are by definition a cheap labor force, but in Ukraine this kind of labor is currently in abundance, so foreigners are often just squeezing out locals from the food markets and from shadow trading businesses, which causes resentment among the population. Migrants also consume social expenditures intended for local citizens—according to estimates, each illegal migrant costs the country \$600–\$800 per year.[17]

16. Hanna Lukanska, 'Violators of virtual borders are not prosecuted'.

17. Olexandr Khomra. 'Illegal Transit Migration as a Threat to the National Security of Ukraine'.

In general, growing illegal migration to Ukraine contributes to the growth of criminality and corruption, and to overloaded social support systems and infrastructures. It threatens cultural identity and can bring social and ethnic tensions. It is not a fantasy any more to conclude that illegal migrants could well have terrorist backgrounds and intentions. In the end, the settling of illegal migrants in Ukraine does not support the economic development of the country (unlike the case of the European Union, where cheap labor is in demand), and it generally threatens Ukraine's relationship with the EU in the future.

Ukraine's improving economy and ever-closer proximity to the enlarging European Union are likely to increase the chances of the country becoming either a desired or involuntary target (a "settling zone") for illegal migrants in the near future. Once the EU is enlarged, and Ukraine's borders with Poland, Slovakia, Hungary, and Romania become much more difficult to penetrate, this will definitely aggravate the problem.

## UKRAINE AS A DONOR OF ILLEGAL MIGRANTS

Ukrainians are travelling to the West and becoming illegal migrants there as well. However, the major difference that distinguishes this kind of illegal labor migration from illegal transit migration through Ukraine is that Ukrainians usually leave their country not for permanent residence in the West, or in Russia, but in order to work there and return home later. There are estimates that they send home around $400 million every year, though the real figure is certainly higher, because not all money is delivered through bank transfers.

However, there are no clear statistics on illegal migration by Ukrainian nationals. Ukrainian authorities admit to a significant discrepancy between the official statistics on the number of Ukrainians working abroad—some 20,000–30,000 every year in the period 2000–2002—and other official estimates, which put this number at around 500,000.[18] According to Ukrainian Ministry of Foreign Affairs estimates, there are up to 3 million Ukrainians working abroad. Of

18. 'Letter of the Ministry of Labour and Social Policy of Ukraine', *Fourth wave of migration: Regional specifics* (Kiev, Institute of Diaspora Studies 2002), p. 36.

this number the highest share are in Russia—1 million, then Poland—300,000, Italy—200,000, Czech Republic—100,000–200,000, Spain—100,000, Turkey—35,000, and the US—20,000. Independent experts' estimate of the total number of Ukrainians working abroad is higher—in excess of 4.5 million (Central Europe—400,000,[19] Western Europe—1.1 million,[20] Russia—over 2.5 million)[21] and sometimes as high as 7 million, when seasonal workers are taken into account.

It is not a big secret that quite a large number of Ukrainian citizens are engaged in illegal labor migration. According to the 2 April 2003 special report of the Ukrainian Parliamentary Commissioner for Human Rights Nina Karpacheva, over the past 2 years over 23,000 Ukrainians were deported home from all over the world. The largest numbers of Ukrainians were deported from Turkey, Hungary, Poland, Slovakia, and Italy. The Ukrainian Foreign Ministry considers the number of Ukrainians illegally living abroad to be 2 million.[22] For instance, in the Czech Republic the quota for Ukrainians is 60,000 (in accordance with a 1996 bilateral agreement), while the actual number of Ukrainians working there and not covered by any social protection is three times higher, which creates fertile ground for numerous abuses and criminal offenses against Ukrainians. However, in this and similar cases, the major problem is not so much reducing the scale of Ukrainian labor migration, but increasing efforts for the legalisation of Ukraine's work force and the adequate protection of the social and human rights of Ukrainian workers abroad. The first relevant agreement "legalizing" Ukrainian workers was signed between Ukraine and Portugal in 2003. Similar agreements are being negotiated with Greece, Italy, Spain, and a few other countries.

A tendency is being observed for Ukrainian workers to leave neighboring Central European countries and go in greater numbers

---

19. Borys Tarasiuk, 'Ukraine's Position in Integrating Europe'. *Immediate Neighbourhood of Ukraine and EU* (Uzhgorod, Valeriy Padiak Publishers 2002) p. 15.

20. Victor Pedenko, *Fourth wave of migration: Regional specifics* (Kiev, Institute of Diaspora Studies 2002), p. 36.

21. Olena Malynovska, *Fourth wave of migration: Regional specifics.* (Kiev, Institute of Diaspora Studies 2002), p.15.

22. Petro Burkovsky, 'Slogan of 2003: Everybody goes working abroad', *Polityka i Kultura*, 11–17 January 2003.

to work in Portugal, Spain, Italy, and Greece, where the attitude of employers and pay are seemingly better.

There is also a specific dimension of illegal migration from Ukraine called trafficking of human beings, which needs to be distinguished from the general illegal migration phenomenon and addressed separately because of its grave social danger—the direct targeting of young women and children for sexual slavery, the pornography industry, and transplants.

As far as the problem of trafficking of human beings is concerned, Ukraine is a typical donor country. General estimates of the IOM, as well as of Ukrainian official structures and NGOs, give the following figures: over 400,000 Ukrainian women under 30 years of age left the country during the past 10 years; some 100,000 of them became sexual slaves; around 25% of Israeli prostitutes, as well as 25% of Turkish prostitutes are from Ukraine; the most popular destination countries for trafficking of Ukrainian girls are Hungary, Czech Republic, Germany, Turkey, Italy, and the US.[23] They are transported through elaborate trafficking networks including fake travel agencies, corrupt officials, and criminal organizations.[24] According to the Ukrainian Foreign Ministry, in 2002, only 213 Ukrainian women were freed from sexual slavery,[25] while according to Security Service data, since 1998 over 400 women returned safely home, of which 28 were under age.[26]

The first meaningful reaction of Ukrainian authorities to this problem came in 1998, when the Ukrainian Parliament introduced severe criminal punishments for trafficking in human beings. From

23. See: Winrock International Ukraine, *Improvement of Ukraine's legislature to prevent trafficking in people*, analytical package for the parliamentary hearings of 18 March 2003.

24. According to a EUROPOL report: 'People smuggling has become the preferred trade of a growing number of criminal networks world-wide which are showing an increasing sophistication in regard to move larger numbers of people at higher profits than ever.... People smuggling syndicates are still benefiting from weak legislation, huge profits and the relatively low risk of detection, prosecution and arrest compared to other activities of transnational organised crime'. See: people smuggling, http://ue.eu.int/pressData/en/misc/70413.pdf.

25. Petro Burkovsky, 'Slogan of 2003: Everybody goes working abroad'. *Polityka i Kultura*, 11–17 January 2003.

26. Expert Centre, 21 April 2003. Ukrainian women were trafficked to Turkey every month in hundreds: http://www.expert.org.ua.

1998 until 2003 over 300 criminal trafficking organizations were exposed. The number of criminal cases initiated against traffickers is growing: 2 cases in 1998, 11 in 1999, 42 in 2000, 91 in 2001, and 169 in 2002. Over 50 of these cases have already been brought to trial, with varying sentences for 250 persons (both Ukrainian and foreign nationals), often in the range of 8–9 years in prison.

Certain organizational measures are also being taken. In 1999, the National Coordination Council for Prevention of Trafficking in People, under the authority of the Ukrainian Parliamentary Commissioner for Human Rights, was established and the Cabinet of Ministers adopted an elaborate government program for the period 1999–2001 for the prevention of trafficking in women and children. In 2002, a similar program was adopted for the period 2002–2005, which improves the methods of combating trafficking through increased investigative efforts against criminals, and envisages the improvement of services for victims, including counselling and shelter. In 2000, anti-trafficking divisions were created in the structure of the Ministry of Internal Affairs.

Unfortunately, so far the introduction of harsher penalties and organizational efforts has yet to affect the problem in any positive way. Ukraine still remains at the top of international lists of contemporary human slave donors. The country is also a concern in terms of the problem of organ trafficking. According to the U.S. Department of State 2003 report:

> Ukraine is a source country for women and girls trafficked to Central and Western Europe and the Middle East for purposes of sexual exploitation. . . . The growth of internal trafficking of young girls is a rising concern, as is the susceptibility of children in orphanages to traffickers. . . . The Government of Ukraine does not yet fully comply with minimum standards for the elimination of trafficking; however, it is making significant efforts to do so. In the past year, the government has shown an effort to sustain and improve existing anti-trafficking structures and mechanisms and increase the ability to prosecute and convict traffickers. Inconsistent cooperation between central government authorities and varying levels of corruption impeded some of the government's planned efforts.[27]

27. U.S. Department of State. 'Victims of Trafficking and Violence Protection Act of 2000: Trafficking in Persons Report', 11 June 2003, http://www.state.gov/g/tip/rls/tiprpt/2003/. 25

In addition, delays in ratifying important international treaties in the area of fighting organized crime also limit the power of authorities to prosecute traffickers. To name but one of the most visible cases: in December 2000 Ukraine signed the first UN Treaty against Transnational Organised Crime, which allows for a more effective fight against trafficking from Ukraine beyond Ukraine's borders. But this treaty has not yet been ratified by Ukraine, because it took over 2 years simply for the joint working group to start the development of the necessary amendments to Ukraine's legislation.

## CONCLUSIONS

The problem of illegal migration in Ukraine, as well as in the wider regional context, is very complex. It involves many national and international actors. A solution to this problem is possible only through a multi-faceted approach. National and international cooperation at all levels is thus of great importance, and one of its most important elements is effective cooperation between neighboring countries.

The economic development of Ukraine and a reduction in the level of corruption will be vital in the resolution of many current problems related to illegal migration including a lack of financial resources to curb illegal transit migration, high incentives for Ukrainian nationals to work abroad illegally, and a lack of alternatives for Ukrainian women.

Fortunately for Ukraine, its problems in fighting illegal migration have brought particular attention to this threat on the part of influential countries of Europe and North America and from international organizations like the UN, NATO, OSCE, IOM, and the European Union. This allows one to hope that the challenge will be diminished after all. Given the relative weakness of the Ukrainian state and other states in the region, international support will continue to have an important role to play in responding to illegal migration.

However, the main problems provoking illegal migration through and from Ukraine (e.g., violent conflicts, tyranny, poverty) are very often impossible to resolve quickly, which means that the challenge cannot easily be dealt with within Ukraine alone, despite the best national and international efforts.

If the European Union's enlargement policy is not substantially modified, Ukraine is likely to remain the EU's "neighbor" for at least a decade and probably a longer period. A lack of progress in resolving the illegal migration issue sooner rather than later, might therefore create a bizarre situation, when "Fortress Europe" becomes besieged for an indefinite time by thousands of migrants trying to cross the Ukrainian border with the EU. As historical experience proves, simply building new walls is not the optimal way to guarantee good security.

# ILLEGAL MIGRATION: RUSSIA

IRINA IVAKHNIOUK

When speaking about illegal migration in terms of regional security threats in Europe it is necessary to realize the shift in the European international migration situation that has happened as a result of the disintegration of the USSR and the collapse of the socialist block.

Russia is usually regarded by the enlarging European Union as a peripheral zone for the exodus of migrants heading to Western European countries as well as to Central European ones. That is true. These migration flows have already created an immigration community in Europe and turned such countries as Poland, the Czech Republic and Hungary into new destination and transit territories.

However, this statement by itself is not enough to understand the current trends and perspectives of international migration in the region.

In terms of international migration systems concepts[1] the vast territory of the former Soviet Union can be regarded as a new international migration system centred on Russia. A migration system is "a group of countries that exchange relatively large numbers of migrants with each other."[2] Migration flows within a migration system are usually centred on one or several destination countries, while the system is open, that is, it has migration links with outside countries and other migration systems as well. Usually, the four major migration systems are identified as the North American, European, Gulf, and Asia-Pacific.[3] Presently, the Euro-Asian migration system must be added to this list, first of all due to the large scale of international migration movements both within the ex-USSR and to and from other countries of the world. Gross non-return migration between former Soviet states in 1992–2001 was over 20 million, and net migration to Russia from other countries of the region was +4.4 million persons.[4]

Being a center of a new migration system Russia acts as a *sending* and—to a much greater extent—as a *receiving* and *transit* country. According to the United Nations classification, in the 1990s Russia was in second place in the world hierarchy of receiving countries after the US, with a total of 12.5 million immigrants.[5] Though Russia's national statistics data differ from the UN criterion of *foreign-born persons*, the total number of immigrants to Russia in 1992—2001 was 10.7 million (including 6.5 million officially registered as "arrived for permanent residence"; 1.2 million refugees; 3 million non-status immigrants)[6] - they

---

1. See, for example, Kritz M., Lean Lim L., Zlotnik H. (eds), *International Migration Systems: A Global Approach* (Oxford: Clarendon Press 1992).
2. Ibid., p. 2.
3. Simmons Alain, Piche Victor, 'Teaching Migration and Globalisation' *Genus*, vol. LVIII no. 3–4, 2002), p. 116.
4. Goskomstat, *Russia's Statistical Yearbook 2001* (Moscow: Goskomstat 2002).
5. United Nations, International Migration (UN: New York, October 2002).
6. 'Non-status immigrants' are not illegal migrants in Russia. This category has appeared as a result of transparent borders between former Soviet states when people who moved to Russia at the beginning of the 1990s and who succeeded in living and working there for years, could not obtain Russian citizenship due to poor legislation.

also confirm Russia's second position among the major receiving countries of the world.[7]

During this rather short period of time Russia has faced a variety of international migration flows including migrations for permanent residence, forced migrant inflow, temporary labor migrations, transit migrations, and illegal migrations. Large-scale migration can be a challenge to national and regional stability by itself as it causes economic, social, ethnic, and other problems, primarily in receiving societies. However, when a large proportion of international migration to a region, within a region, through a region, and out of a region is taking place in a non-controlled, illegal form it carries threats to regional and international security. That is the case in the Euro-Asian migration system.

Europe's interest in migration in the ex-USSR is clear. Since the expanding European Union will have Russia as its close neighbor, it should be interested in finding out what this neighbor is like. Naturally, knowing the neighbor living next door is very important for your own well-being. If your neighbour is calm, friendly and successful then you can feel secure. But if your neighbour is hostile, secretive and has a household full of strange, suspicious guests, then there are grounds for concern.

In Russia, illegal migration has become an issue of political and public debate. It is not an exaggeration to say that among the problems related to international migration, illegal migration and its effects on Russia's economy and society are the most obvious at the government level, among experts and in the media. The point of view that illegal migration is to be considered in the context of national security has become dominant after the Russian Federation Security Council declared in 2001 that the scale of illegal immigration had grown into a real threat to national security. For this reason the general tone of the illegal migration debate is obviously negative.

To provide effective management of any social process it is crucially important to understand its nature and scale; to break the process down into its component parts is desirable. In the case of illegal

7. Iontsev, Vladimir and Ivakhniouk, Irina, 'Russia in World Migration Flows: Trends of the Last Decade (1992–2001)' in 'World in the Mirror of International Migration', scientific series *International Migration: Russia and the Contemporary World* Volume 10 (Moscow: MAX Press 2002) p. 52 (in Russian).

migration, only the understanding of its diverse multiply structure can lead the way to a complex multi-level approach to managing its challenges.

## SCALE OF THE PROBLEM

In any country, estimation of the number of illegal immigrants can be based on indirect data and experts' estimates only. However, in Russia, the range of estimations is impressive.

When during the same week Boris Gryzlov, head of the Ministry of Internal Affairs responsible for migration regulation, has mentioned that there are 1.5 million illegal migrants in the country,[8] while Alexander Chernenko, head of the Federal Migration Service acting within the same ministry declared that the number of illegal migrants in Russia exceeds 6 million,[9] it is evident that even senior officials have little idea of the scale of the phenomenon they are to manage with.

Inspired with such an irresponsibility of estimations, journalists feel free to give their own estimates up to 15 million[10] as the total number of illegal migrants and over 3 million in the Moscow region alone.[11]

Even experts' estimates differ greatly. For example, Galina Vitkovskaya, coordinator of the International Organisation for Migration (IOM) Moscow Migration Research Program, gives an estimate of 3 million,[12] Zhanna Zayonchkovskaya, head of the Migration Analysis and Forecasting Laboratory at the Russian Academy of Sciences' (RAS) Institute of National-Economic Forecasting—3–4 million,[13] Yevgeniy Krasinets, expert on illegal migration at the RAS

8. ITAR-TASS News Agency, 12 December 2002.

9. Paper presented by Alexandr Chernenko at the State Duma hearings on Russia's Migration Policy Concept on 9 December 2002.

10. *Gazeta*, 12 March 2003.

11. *Vremya MN*, 12 December 2002.

12. Galina Vitkovskaya 'Irregular Migration in Russia: Situation and Policy of Counteraction' in Illegal Immigration. Scientific series *International Migration: Russia and the Contemporary World* Volume 9 (Moscow: MAX Press 2002) (in Russian).

13. IOM *Irregular Migration in Russia: Opening the Debate*, IOM Open Forum, Moscow Migration Research Programme Information Series, No. 1, 2001.

Institute for Socio-Economic Studies of Population—4–4.5 million.[14] V. Ivanov, head of the Presidential Committee on Migration Policy, said that if no urgent measures to combat illegal migration were undertaken, it will increase threefold by 2010—up to 19 million. This figure was multi-copied by the media.[15]

Putting aside extreme estimations provoked either by panicked inspirations or by political maneuvers, we prefer to analyze illegal migration in Russia by categories:

1. The most numerous category of illegal migrants in Russia are citizens of the ex-USSR countries who come to Russia in quest of jobs and/or residence. Visa-free regimes based on bilateral agreements between the majority of CIS countries[16] allow them to cross the boundaries legally. However, due to bureaucratic obstacles on the way to Russian citizenship and legal employment the overwhelming majority of migrants find themselves illegal in status. They are primarily employed in the informal sector of the economy. Their number is rapidly growing. Now it can be estimated at 3–4 million.
2. Hundreds of thousands of refugees from Afghanistan, Somalia, Ethiopia, Turkey, Sri Lanka, Angola, and other countries reached Russia after the country signed the 1951 UN Convention on Refugees and its supplementary 1967 Protocol in 1992. Only some of them were granted refugee status, while the others preferred to move to the West for better living standards or to stay in Russia illegally. They number over 200,000.
3. Transit migrants from Asian and African countries arrive with transit visas and head towards Western Europe where they intend to apply for refugee status or join their relatives. They lose their legal transit migrant status when they overstay the transit term. They often "get lost" in the vast territories of Russia for years. Their number is around 500,000.

14. Krasinets Yevgeniy, Kubishin Yelena, Tiuriukanova Yelena *Illegal migration to Russia* (Moscow: Academia, 2000) p. 82.

15. See, for example, Chuykin M. 'Russia Is Becoming a Heaven for Illegal Migrants', *Nezavisimaya Gazeta*, 5 February 1999 (in Russian).

16. Russia has signed agreements on visa-free entry with all the CIS states except Georgia and Turkmenistan.

4. Foreign citizens who after the end of contract work in Russia (mainly from Vietnam and Korea) or after graduating from Russian universities and professional schools (from, for example, Afghanistan, Iraq, Cuba, Congo, Guinea, and Ethiopia) prefer not to return to their countries but to stay in Russia. They are about 80,000.
5. Migrants who enter the country illegally, without border control or with false documents. Their arrival can be related to illegal transit towards the West, or short-term stay in Russia for criminal reasons. Very approximately they can be estimated at 100,000–150,000.

Thus, the total number of illegal migrants in Russia can be estimated at 4–5 million. We have reasons to suppose that the existing restricting trend in migration regulation can provoke the growth of illegal migration. For example, it was estimated that a 25-times increase in fees for employers hiring foreign workers in 2002 would only push migrant workers into illegality.[17]

## 'ILLEGAL' MIGRANTS FROM THE FORMER SOVIET STATES

The majority of illegal migrants in Russia are citizens of the former Soviet states (defined in Russia as "new foreign states" in contradistinction to the "old foreign states," or traditionally understood foreign countries). Usually they come to Russia in quest of jobs, so this migration flow is labor migration by nature. Its illegal form is determined by an artificially narrowed (by poor legislation) field for legal labor migration. Moreover, the significant part of these "illegal" migrants (I put illegal in quotes because in fact they are forced to be illegal migrants) would prefer to be legal migrant workers; however, they live in Russia for years or arrive to work regularly and *cannot* legalize their status.

Can these people be regarded as a threat to Russia's national security? Yes, to a certain extent: they are out of the official statistics and employment systems, they do not pay taxes and do not have access to the social security system. Usually these migrant workers are employed in the informal sector (construction, trade and shadow

17. *Vremya Novostei*, 25 April 2002.

production, e.g., clandestine factories, illegal services). Experts estimate the shadow sector of Russia's economy at a quarter of GNP, and employment in it at 15–30% of the total labor force.[18] The concentration of illegal migrants in local labor markets provokes ethnic-based tension and migrantophobia.

The negative effects of illegal migration are well known: they are typical for all countries that cope with it. For Russia, the "negative degree" of these effects is maybe even higher because illegal migrants disorganise a national labor market that is on the path to market economy; they increase illegal employment "niches" and, consequently, impede the transition process. Thus, large-scale illegal labor migration from new foreign states is an obvious threat to Russia's economic security.

Regretfully, the reaction of Russian authorities to the negative effects of illegal migration spreads to international migration as a whole. This results in the restrictive character of migration regulation, focused on migration control enforcement and working out mechanisms of deportation. Alternative measures, such as legalization of migrants and widening of the legal field for migration, are out of sight of government bodies responsible for migration regulation.

However, the present trends of economic and demographic development of Russia necessitate different views on migration inflow (both legal and illegal). Already now Russia is in need of an additional labor force. According to national statistical data, in 2000, 6% of enterprises in Russia faced a labor deficit; by 2002 it was 30%.[19] The labor shortage is especially noticeable in the Ural Region where big factories are located: now they are in the process of recovery. The demographic trends will worsen the situation in the next few years: after 2006 the steady decrease in labor-active age groups will start, due to the existing age structure and low fertility. The long-term demographic perspective is distressing: by 2050 Russia's population will be probably not more than 90 million (40% less than

---

18. Radayev V. 'Shadow Economy of Russia. Reshaping of Contours', *Pro et Contra*, Winter 1999, p. 10 (in Russian).

19. Zayonchkovskaya, Zhanna Labour Immigration from the CIS countries to Russia. Paper presented at the IOM/ILO Conference 'Labour Markets and Labour Immigration in Russia: Demand, Offer and Reaction of the Accepting Society', Moscow, 29 November 2002.

the current number), labor age groups will decline from 60% to 47%, while those over 60 years will more than double: from 20% to 43%.[20] These figures emphasize Russia's need of migrants. Labour demand will necessarily cause labor migration inflow. The question is, whether foreign labor comes to Russia's labor market on a legal basis or on an illegal basis. The answer strongly depends on a migration policy concept that would not run contrary to the country's economic and demographic interests.

Annually, over 300,000 foreign workers are officially employed in Russia. However, this data reflects only the tip of an iceberg: the number of illegal workers is not less that tenfold higher. This demonstrates the high labor migration potential in the neighboring countries. Given a regulative but not restrictive government labor migration policy, Russia can benefit from this potential.

Besides, illegal labor migration from ex-USSR countries has invisible effects related to Russia's national security. A paradox but a fact: receiving illegal migrants in its territory Russia is in a way providing itself with "safe borders" with other former Soviet states. By earning money in Russia illegal migrants from Azerbaijan, Armenia, and Central Asian countries are supporting their families at home where the economic situation is much worse and therefore they help avoid possible social outbursts. The current slackening of ethnic tension and anti-Russian trends are not by chance: these countries are once again becoming dependent on Russia; however, in a totally different aspect than before.

## EURO-ASIAN ILLEGAL TRANSIT

The most "irritating" issue in the context of European security threats in the migration sphere is Russia's new position as a Euro-Asian transit corridor for numerous overt and covert routes from Asian and African countries to Europe.

The attractiveness of Russia as a transit "staging post" for (mainly illegal) migrants is determined by the relatively transparent borders within the post-Soviet territory (in combination with agreements

20. Vishnevskiy, Anatoliy ed. *Population of Russia 2001 Annual Demographic Report.* (Moscow: Goskomstat) pp. 182–193 (in Russian).

on visa-free entry with third countries that were signed by some CIS states[21] it provides a rather comfortable and cheap land route for transit migrants from Asia to Russia or for onward travel to the West); poor legislation regulating foreigners' entry, residence, and employment in Russia; and disorganization of the domestic labor market, with a significant informal sector, whence irregular migrants most often derive their income.

Other important factors are Russia's geographic location, which stands between Asia and Europe, and its intermediate economic position between developed and developing countries that makes it a natural channel for migrants from developing countries. According to Ministry of Internal Affairs statistics, at the present time there are over 300,000 transit migrants from Afghanistan, China, Angola, Pakistan, India, Sri Lanka, Turkey, Ethiopia, and other countries "stuck" in Russia.[22] Besides, there is a significant flow of migrants who illegally penetrate Russian borders trying to reach EU countries.

The presence of illegal/irregular transit migrants in Russia is incompatible with the national interests of the country. Many of these migrants are involved in crime and the places where they concentrate become sources of exotic infectious diseases, drug addiction, and prostitution.

It is admittedly unfortunate that, until now, Russian official structures did not manage to properly control the arrival and stay of transit migrants in the country. After entering with a transit or tourist visa (or crossing the border illegally) they usually escape from migration service control. The 2000 initiatives[23] directed at enforcement of migration control, and organization of regional migration information

---

21. For example, there are agreements on visa-free entry between China and Kyrgyzstan and between Kyrgyzstan and Kazakhstan and between Kazakhstan and Russia. Sadovskaya, Yelena 'Prevention of Irregular Migration in Kazakhstan' Illegal Immigration. Series *International Migration of Population: Russia and the Contemporary World* Vol. 9, 2002 (Moscow, MAX Press) p. 51 (in Russian).

22. IOM *Management of Migration in the CIS Countries: Legislation and Cross-Border Cooperation*, IOM Open Forum, Moscow Migration Research Programme Information Series (Special Issue No. 3) p. 4.

23. On 25 January 2000, the parties to the CIS Agreement on Combating Illegal Migration in the Region (signed on 6 March 1998) agreed to organize a common database on illegal migrants and other "unwanted persons." Russia was declared coordinating country for implementation of this initiative.

and analytical centers and the united migration database have good potential to improve the situation.

However, at the present moment it is much easier for transit migrants to enter Russia than to leave it. It is a widespread misapprehension that the transparency of Russian borders with other CIS states is the major attractive feature of Russia for transit migrants. Over 80% of migrants come to Russia legally with valid passports and visas (for transit, tourism, private reasons, business, study, or work). They become illegal migrants later, when they overstay their permitted term, change passports for forged ones, fake visas, and so on. Lack of control over migrants in Russia allows them to stay in the country for their purposes (e.g., to earn money, to wait for other members of a group) quite safely for a long period of time.

However, the CIS' western frontiers in Russia, Belarus, and Ukraine are controlled much more strictly than its eastern frontiers. By prohibiting the illegal exit of those migrants who have violated the terms of their visas, or have used forged documents, for example, the Russian frontier services are in fact turning Russia into a "settling tank" for illegal migrants. As a result, transit lasts for years, and a transit migrant turns into illegal migrant and most often finds himself or herself in a socially dangerous criminal environment.

Here, we face a crucially important issue: transit illegal migrants are not "independent" in Russia, that is, they do not act by themselves. They are managed by well-organized criminal structures specializing in migrant smuggling. In general, illegal migration is no longer a spontaneous process. It is a well organized and extremely profitable business with low risks. According to a number of estimates, the overall annual profit from the smuggling of migrants in the world is $5–7 billion.

## SMUGGLING AND TRAFFICKING BUSINESS

After the post-Soviet territory became open for international migrations it became a sphere of particular interest for the global migrant smuggling network. Along the borders of Russia, especially on the Russian-Chinese, Russian-Kazakh, and Russian-Ukrainian borders, there exist numerous channels for migrant smuggling. (90% of illegal migration to Russia comes from Kazakhstan, where there are almost 7600 km of practically open border.)

International criminal networks specializing in smuggling of migrants and trafficking in migrants control the majority of legal and illegal labor recruiting agencies, marriage bureaus, visa brokers, and other intermediaries involved in the international migration business. They have stable contacts in migrants' countries of origin, transit, and destination and provide a wide range of services related to legal or illegal border crossing. This means that in counteracting illegal migration the state is facing not individual migrants but a strong criminal structure. The Russian segment of this structure is technically advanced (this is obviously seen from high-quality forged passports, stamps, documents, invitations, visas, etc.) and flexible (it easily adjusts its activities in accordance with changes in the situation at border crossing points). Besides, their activity is usually diversified: migrant smuggling channels often coincide with drugs trafficking and weapons transfer channels.

At least two major conclusions are to be made from understanding of this fact:

(1) efforts to combat regional and national security threats should be focused not on illegal migration by itself but on those structures which are managing it;
(2) there should be coordinated and combined efforts of all the countries concerned by the negative effects of illegal migration at international and regional levels.

Over the past five years, the number of those detained at Russian borders has increased almost tenfold. This figure includes citizens of thirty countries with which Russia shares no common border. In 1999–2000, the Russian Federal Frontier Service, together with law-enforcement agencies, detained more than 2000 irregular migrants and exposed about 400 criminal groups specializing in moving irregular migrants.[24]

This activity of the Russian law-enforcement agencies is primarily aimed at protecting Russia's interests and its national security while simultaneously safeguarding the interests of those transit migrants' target countries. It would be logical to assume that common interests need common efforts (in the framework of information exchange,

24. IOM *Irregular Migration in Russia: Opening the Debate*, IOM Open Forum, Moscow Migration Research Programme Information Series, No. 1, 2001, p. 3.

international agreements counteracting illegal migration, etc.). If European countries are interested in preventing illegal migration "from afar"—as they should—then they should become the initiators of international programs and agreements in this domain, of joint scientific projects in international migration in the context of soft security threats and of in-depth studies on the most topical issues (for example, the prospects of cross-border cooperation in preventing illegal migration; the impact of Russian temporary irregular labor migrants on EU candidate countries' industries; human trafficking in the CIS region).

We should keep in mind that illegal migration—like international migration of people in general—is a supra-national phenomenon. To regulate it, combined international efforts of all the countries involved are needed. Otherwise this supra-national character will contradict national regulating concepts. This can cause what has been called a crisis of management, that is, loss of control over migrations (the case of Russia proves that). The growth of the scale of illegal migration is a result of this process.

## CHINESE MIGRATION

Chinese migration needs special emphasis in the context of the migration threats debate. In fact, Chinese migration can be regarded as a challenge not only to Russia's national security but to the security of many regions of the world. It is strange, for example, that the Western world is concerned with potential threats of Muslim or Arabic migration but practically ignores the challenge of Chinese migration that can mean a serious shift in the global political situation in future.[25]

For Russia, Chinese migration is an extremely topical issue. First, Chinese migrants are the most numerous foreign population group after Ukrainians in the country. Second, in this case the Russian state is again dealing with activity organized, inspired, and managed by the Chinese government. For China, Russia is not simply the nearest

25. The distinguished American economist and demographer Paul Demeny is one of the few Western scholars who broaches this question in: 'Prospects for International Migration: Globalization and Its Discontents', *Journal of Population Research*, Vol. 19, No. 1, 2002, pp. 65–67.

neighbor with an extensive common border. Russia's geopolitical location determines its significant role in Beijing's strategy, in particular the new external economic strategy declared at the Third Session of the All-Chinese Assembly in spring 2000. This strategy has gained popularity as the slogan "To go outside."[26] One of the goals of the strategy is to provide a breakthrough to world markets, including the international labor market, and to support economic progress in China by means of other countries' raw materials and financial resources. The growing Chinese migration and activities of Chinese ethnic communities all over the world are to play a crucial role in realization of this strategy.

In this context Russia is regarded, first, as a suitable field for economic activities of hundreds of thousands of Chinese migrants; second, as an inexhaustible source of raw materials (for example, timber and metals necessary for Chinese industries); third, as a staging post for Chinese migrants on their way to western countries. For the present, the total number of Chinese migrants who live in Russia more or less permanently is about half a million (the most reasonable estimate from a long row of existing estimates).[27] However, this figure will inevitably grow along with the process of Russia's economic recovery.

The most important factor is a huge difference in demographic potential on the two sides of the Russian-Chinese border. Population in three Chinese provinces neighboring Russia's Far East exceeds 110 million and population density is 130 per square kilometer, while in four Russian administrative regions close to the border—the Jewish Autonomous Region, Amur Region, Primorskiy Region, and Khabarovsk Territory—population density is only 4 per square kilometer, and the number of citizens is less than 6 million. Moreover, during the last decade outflow of population from these Far East regions to the central parts of the country was over 1 million: every sixth citizen has departed. This demographic disproportion alone can be a strong reason for the flow of China's population through

26. Ghelbras, Vilia 'Chinese Migration and Chinese Communities in Russia' in 'The World in the Mirror of International Migration'. Scientific series *International Migration: Russia and the Contemporary World* Vol. 10 (Moscow: MAX Press 2002) (in Russian).

27. Ghelbras, Vilia *The Chinese Reality of Russia. Moscow* (Moscow: Muravey Publishing House 2001) (in Russian).

the Russian boundary. One forecast argues that by the mid-21st century Chinese people in Russia will number 8–10 million, so they will be the second largest ethnic group in Russia after Russians.[28]

When at the beginning of the 1990s Russian territory was opened for Chinese labor migrants[29] it resulted in large-scale (poorly controlled) migration to the Russia's Far East. That hasty agreement has brought many labor migrants to Russia as well as people whose ultimate goal is to reach Western Europe via Russian territory. Many migrants stayed in Russia as irregular migrants. Even after the open border policy was cancelled in 1994, the floodgate of Chinese migration was not closed completely: it became primarily illegal.

Gradual settlement of Russia's Far East by Chinese people is silently encouraged by the Chinese government. It continues to hold the 'lost territories concept': according to it 1.5 million hectares of Chinese territory has been 'seized' by Tsarist Russia. In the modern geographical school maps a major part of Russia's Far East Region is included in the borders of China.

The situation is complicated by the fact that for the first time in the history of relations between Russia and China the latter is stronger economically: all the diagrams of economic, financial, demographic development of China show an upward trend since the beginning of the 1990s.[30] Rapid economic development of China, with the world's largest population, can affect the correlation of forces in the Euro-Asian region and shift the political balance in the world. Insufficient attention of the Russian federal authorities towards problems related to Chinese migration to Russia's Far East (as well as to the economic prospects of the region) is resulting in the fact that this vast territory of Russia has become the weakest section in its national security system.

The 2001 agreement on good-neighbourliness between Russia and China includes statements concerning the necessity to prevent illegal migration, and illegal transit in particular. However, real

28. Verlin, Yevgeniy '"Black Cash" and Yellow Danger', *Expert* No. 11, 18 March 2002 (in Russian).

29. Inter-Governmental Agreement Between the Russian Federation and the People's Republic of China "On principles of employment of Chinese citizens in enterprises and organizations in Russia" signed on 19 August 1992.

30. Rudakov, A. Voskresenskiy, A. 'Shadow of China', *Profil*, February 2002 (in Russian).

measures to combat illegal migration are not detailed, neither are bilateral measures to provide a legislative framework for legal migration.

The supporting element for Chinese illegal migration in Russia (as well as worldwide) are Chinese ethnic communities. In a number of Russian cities they have developed into strong independent economic and social structures, enclaves in Russia's economy. Having at their disposal the community's independent press, financial system, various legal and semi-legal companies, hotels, hostels, warehouses, etc., the Chinese ethnic communities have become the coordinating centers for Chinese migrants' business activities.

Chinese tourist agencies in Russia accumulate significant financial resources by monopolizing services for Chinese migrants who arrive in Russia. On their route Chinese tourists are transported by buses and cars that belong to Chinese companies, have meals in Chinese restaurants, are accompanied by Chinese guides, and so on. To shop, a Chinese tourist may change yuan or dollars for rubles exclusively from the group leader or the guide. As a result the money spent by tourists in Russia mainly stays in the Chinese community or returns to China. Here is only one piece of evidence: the Chinese bank "Elos" that is operating in Moscow, exceeds the biggest Russian bank "Sberbank" in the amount of accumulated hard currency from non-Russian citizens.[31]

Within the Chinese community in Moscow there have developed semi-legal agencies dealing with invitations and visa support for Chinese people who would like to migrate to Russia or to other countries using Russia as a transit stage. In Chinese papers published in Moscow one can easily find advertisements for companies who openly offer smuggling of Chinese migrants to Schengen countries, Canada, Australia, South Africa, and Latin America.[32] Thus, the Chinese intermediaries feel comfortable in Russia: they operate with significant financial resources, use corrupt officials, and succeed in finding weak points in Russia's border control.

31. Information from Vilia Ghelbras, the distinguished Russian expert in Chinese migration (see: *Irregular Migration in Russia: Opening the Debate*, IOM Open Forum, Moscow Migration Research Programme Information Series, No. 1, 2001 p. 5).

32. Ghelbras, Vilia 'Chinese Migration and Chinese Communities in Russia', 'The World in the Mirror of International Migration' Scientific series "*International Migration: Russia and the Contemporary World*" Volume 10, 2002 (Moscow MAX Press) (in Russian).

## COMBATING ILLEGAL MIGRATION: COMPLEX APPROACH

The above arguments prove that while illegal migration is a heterogeneous phenomenon, the measures to prevent it should be multi-level. Illegal migration cannot be defeated by an "administrative storm." Restricting measures should be added to regulating measures. Border control improvement is surely topical for Russia. Development of international instruments, like readmission agreements, is also topical. However, these restrictive measures should not run contrary to the reality resulting from hundreds of thousands of illegal migrants from CIS countries who are *de facto* permanent residents of Russia. A survey of illegal migrants from Ukraine in Moscow in 2000[33] showed that 20% of respondents live in Moscow for over three years; half of them for over five years. The fact that they work and find means of subsistence in Russia proves that the country is in need of them. The fact that they have no legal status is likely to prove that they are forced into that status. A normal man prefers not "to sit on a shaky chair" and pay bribes to put his child into a kindergarten, school, or hospital. Meanwhile, complicated bureaucratic procedures related to registration, citizenship, or even labor contracts leave many of these migrants on an illegal field. In fact, the state itself is becoming the reason for growing illegal migration.

The undeveloped and inadequate state of national legislation on migration improperly narrows the scope of legitimate migration and consequently broadens the scope of irregular and illegal migration. However, migration legislation is not drafted in a vacuum. It is a manifestation of official migration policy. In Russia, the debates on a reasonable concept for a migration policy have been going on for over ten years; however, so far there has been no common attitude towards migration either in society or among policy-makers. Many groups are now calling for a scrutiny of migration policy, especially in the fields of immigration and transit migration. If this entails improved border controls, restrictions on illegal migration and irregular employment, the scrutiny could be regarded as advantageous. However, if it results in restrictions on labor migration and permanent

33. *Immigration Policy of Russia: Ethnic Context.* IOM Open Forum. Moscow Migration Research Programme Information Series, No. 5, 2002, p.18.

immigration to Russia, it can, first, damage national security interests (mostly in the economic and demographic dimensions) and, second, provoke the growth of illegal and uncontrolled migration.

At the same time, since 2000 Russia's official efforts in migration regulation are primarily focused on controlling illegal migration. In late 1999, Russia suspended the procedure for the transit of foreign nationals through Russian territory as provided for under the Agreement on the Mutual Recognition of CIS Member States' Visas, and a year later it withdrew from the Agreement on Visa-Free Movement of CIS Countries' Citizens on the Territory of Its Participants. The reason for these moves is rooted mainly in the turn of migration management towards illegal migration. Before 5 December 2000,[34] Russia had concluded with practically all the CIS member states multilateral and bilateral agreements on reciprocal visa-free travel. Therefore, Russia attempted to balance human rights against the legitimate right of every country or community of countries to secure itself against the threats and challenges posed by irregular/illegal migration. These decisions mainly concerned nationals of third countries who are to obtain entry, exit, and transit visas from each country.

Aided by the CIS Agreement on Cooperation to Control Irregular Migration[35] and the 2000 initiatives of the participants of this agreement directed at developing cross-border cooperation, enforcement of migration control, and organization of regional migration information and analytical centres and a united migration database, the efforts within the CIS have good potential to improve the situation. Russia is crucially interested in implementation of regional cooperation to combat irregular migration. However, at the same time the economic and demographic interests of Russia need an additional labor force, development of a common economic space, and a common labor market. For this reason Russia's long-term strategy in management of migration is to balance these interests against national security threats posed by irregular migration.

For the present, this strategy remains undeveloped. On the one hand, there is still no clear official migration concept in the country. The state position towards different categories of migrants, and the

34. The date of Russia's withdrawal from the Agreement on Visa-Free Movement of CIS Countries' Citizens on the Territory of Its Participants.

35. Signed on 6 March 1998.

migrants' social and legal rights; priorities in granting citizenship and permanent resident status are not defined in the 2002 Law on Legal Status of Foreign Citizens in the Russian Federation, nor in the 2002 Law on Citizenship which actually tightened conditions to become a Russian citizen, even for former Soviet citizens. In fact, these laws demonstrate a restrictive trend. At the same time, despite migration regulation being focused primarily on illegal migration, there is no definition of "illegal/irregular migrant" in the Russian legislation, there are no articles that would envisage punishment for organizing and aiding human trafficking and illegal movement of citizens of third countries through the territory of Russia in the administrative or criminal codes of the Russian Federation.

Perhaps this position is in line with a general change in attitude towards migration in the world. After the 11 September 2001 tragedy, even in the US—the most tolerant country to migrants—appeals to review immigration policy for restriction and to combat illegal migration for the sake of national security have appeared.[36] In fact, the battle against terrorism is turning into an irrational battle against migration in general. The term "migrant" is becoming filled with negative meaning. This can become a very dangerous delusion that will result in restrictive migration policy and consequently it will provoke an increase in illegal migration as always happens when legal ways of migration become closed.

## CONCLUSION

Different aspects of security are not neutral to each other: when they come in contact they can either complement or contradict one another. Thus, to better defend its territorial security, Russia can strengthen border control, tighten immigration policy and finally will succeed in reducing legal and illegal migration inflow. However, given the current demographic crisis and natural population decline, this will surely mean a challenge to its demographic and economic security. At the same time, while immigration to Russia has an input to the demographic security of the nation, it causes certain economic,

36. See, for example, Kritz, Mary 'Time for National Discussion on Immigration', *International Migration Review* Vol. 36, No. 1, Spring 2002, pp. 33–36.

social, criminal, ethnic, and cultural threats to individuals and communities. In their turn, these threats can culminate in a threat to political sustainability and to national security. However, it is not a vicious circle. It is just an illustration of how important it is in the particular circumstances of contemporary Russia to avoid one-sided emotional approaches in migration policy and in a more general sense in foreign policy. The search for a reasonable well-grounded long-term foreign policy that would be in line with the national security concept and regional interests is on the agenda in Russia.

In this context cooperation with the community of international experts—scholars, analysts, high-level practical specialists—is extremely valuable. Large-scale discussions within this community and its dialogue with policy-makers can be effective instruments for managing the challenges to migration security threats.

# HUMAN TRAFFICKING: THE NADIR OF AN UNHOLY TRINITY

ANDREW NICHOLS PRATT

"Soft security" issues and trends directly concern the security and stability of states in Europe and Eurasian region.[1] While a host of topics suggest themselves as regional threats and risks (migration, environmental degradation, demographics, and the political and economic impact of globalization to cite a few), terrorism, corruption, and international organized crime represent today's most pathological threats to the developing democracies in Europe and Eurasia. These three threats can be described as the "unholy trinity of globalization." Furthermore, the pernicious role exercised by international organized crime in human trafficking or the commodification of human beings cannot be underestimated.

While human trafficking is not as obviously lethal as the first-order effects of terrorism, the growth in the wholesale buying and selling of humans, engineered by elements within international criminal organizations, is a putative soft security threat and one that is capable of undermining domestic stability, whether authoritarian or

1. The views expressed in this article are those of the author in his private capacity and do not necessarily represent those of the United States or German governments.

democratically based, if left unchecked. The concomitant corruption that parallels this commodification of human beings further undermines the political and economic aspects of a nation's democratic development, and trafficking alone can destroy the very moral "soul" of a state, its psychological and socio-cultural identity. Of all the threats that affect the Europe-Eurasian region, international organized crime's activities most directly threaten the development of liberal democracies and free markets by fuelling corruption and looting their nascent gross domestic products (GDPs).

All states in Europe and Eurasia experience this problem to some degree. As Ambassador Gary Govan of the Organization for Security and Cooperation in Europe (OSCE) observed: "International organized crime and the corruption that follows big money are not even stopping to knock on the door. They are already inside."[2] Criminal elements that prey at once upon the economic misfortunes of the region and its vulnerable citizens have introduced the nadir of criminal activity into Eurasia—human trafficking. An understanding of why this has occurred is imperative to understanding the nature of the threat.

Relations in our globalizing world, among both new and old nation states have become much more complex. The world is a much more convoluted place without the stabilizing tension of the opposing ideologies of totalitarian communism and free market capitalism.[3] States are no longer arranged like iron filings into an orderly orientation around the two powerful magnets of the past. They are finding novel and peaceful ways to settle old grudges with neighbors as well as looking for innovative ways to interact with immediate neighbors and still-powerful regional players.

Yet, some new magnets tug at them. The new Europe and Eurasian space has proven remarkably open to grim outside influences. The new states are not necessarily weaker than the old ones and an

2. Remarks by Ambassador Gregory G. Govan, United States Ambassador to the OSCE, George C. Marshall European Center for Security Studies, Garmisch-Partenkirchen, Germany, 8 December 2000.

3. Thomas Friedman, *The Lexus and the Olive Tree*, (New York: Anchor Books, 1999), p. 7.

incomplete explanation suggests that we are simply living in different times. However, new malevolent actors such as international organized criminal groups, pose threats for strong governments as well as weaker ones, and thrive because today's societies and economies are open, independent and politically vulnerable.

Simple arithmetic helps explain the remarkable growth of organized crime and its associated political-criminal nexus, the concentration of politically and regionally organized criminal power.[4] The basic factors that influence the emergence of this silent threat are typical elements of human nature: ego, irrationality, intolerance, and aggression. When these basic elements of human nature are combined with certain mega-trends unique to today's globalizing world, sophisticated criminal activity grows like bacteria in a Petri dish. These mega-trends are the current population explosion in lesser-developed countries, the globalization of international trade, the lure of migration where the grass always appears greener in someone else's country and, the overwhelming effect of the information explosion produced by the mass media.

Many regions of the world are experiencing a population explosion, which has resulted in a population/resource imbalance and in the potential destruction of much of our environment. A good example can be found in the Muslim world. Demographically, this region is in a challenging situation and its problems migrate quite literally into Europe and Eurasia. The relative size of the current younger Muslim generation of youth is unprecedented. Most are single, urban males; almost half have not received a secondary education; and, many are unemployed or underemployed. Many states in the world will experience substantial youth bulges over the next two decades and the largest comparative youth populations will be located in Pakistan, Afghanistan, Saudi Arabia, Yemen, and Iraq. Overall, the age structure in the Arab world is significantly younger than the global average. Thirty-eight percent of this population is younger than 14 while only 6 percent is over

4. Roy Godson, *Trends in Organized Crime*, Vol. 4, No. 3. (Spring 1999), p. 1. The National Strategy Information Center, which Roy Godson directs at Georgetown University, first introduced the concept of the political-criminal nexus from the initial findings of an in-depth collaborative cross-national research study.

60 years old. Further exacerbating the problem, the male/female ratio in several Arab states is also tilted heavily toward males, which is a source of individual frustration and contributes to wider social instability. This sexual imbalance is compounded by the accepted practice of men with high social status taking multiple wives, further reducing the number of women available for marriage. In the United Arab Emirates and Qatar, men outnumber women by almost two to one.[5]

Historically, a large cohort of young, unemployed, single males has been linked to increased political instability. Earlier examples include Algeria, Egypt, the Gaza Strip, Iran, and Turkey. Today Eurasia faces a similar problem. This cohort also provides a convenient pool from which to potential terrorists. According to the Central Intelligence Agency, failure to adequately integrate these young males into society in the Middle East and North Africa is likely to perpetuate the ongoing cycle of political instability, ethnic wars, revolutions, and anti-regime activities. Most significantly for Europe and Eurasia, these "extra" males will find their way into international organized crime activities as populations flee repressive regimes and illegal immigrants seek a better and safer region in which to earn a livelihood.[6]

The second mega-trend is the globalizing of international trade, which is a double-edged sword that causes economic growth as well as social-economic disparity. In many regions of the world, man has evolved from "Homo sapiens" to "Homo connectus"; however, this evolution has not been universal.

As Thomas Barnett of the U.S. Naval War College in Newport argued:

> 'Show me where globalization is thick with network connectivity, financial transactions, liberal media flows, and collective security, and I will show you regions featuring stable governments, rising standards of living, and more deaths by suicide than murder. These parts of the world I call the Functioning Core, or Core. But show me where globalization is thinning or just plain absent, and I will show you regions plagued by politically repressive regimes,

5. 'Long-Term Strategy for the Global War on Terrorism', Interim Briefing for the US Deputy Secretary of Defense, by Michael G. Vickers, Director of Strategic Studies, Center for Strategy and Budget Analysis, 11 December 2002, Slide 16.
6. 'Long-Term Strategy for the Global War on Terrorism', Slide 17.

widespread poverty and disease, routine mass murder, and—most important—the chronic conflicts that incubate the next generation of global terrorists. These parts of the world I call the Non-Integrating Gap, or Gap.'[7]

The globalizing of this functioning core is accelerating so quickly that many living on the outside, or in the "Non-Integrating Gap" will not be able to connect. The modern world, defined by where globalization has truly taken root, magnifies the disconnectedness of these Gap areas, where globalization has not taken root. Thus, globalization becomes a source and a vector from which criminal activities flourish and migrate. Homo sapiens realizes how well off Homo connectus subsists and he wants to be part of this world, he wants "part of the action."

The third mega-trend, the myth of migration, describes a situation where the grass is always greener in another country; where illegal immigrants are literally voting with their feet and changing regional demographic balances. The outer border of Europe is hemorrhaging under the relentless waves of illegal immigrants. The bulk of them from Eastern Europe or Asia, enter the European Union without work permits. The political pressures on the frontline states being pounded by these immigration waves are equally formidable. Countries internal within the European Union have to adopt expedient immigration counter measures that are either not in accordance with Les Accords de Schengen (Schengen Agreements) or violate the agreements in spirit.

But the problem is not Europe's alone. Chinese trafficking networks known as "snakehead organizations" ship people from China and other Asian countries to points all over the globe. Paralleling the narcotics trade routes, human traffickers use a combination of air, sea, and land routes and follow similar geographical paths.[8] Because of these trafficking networks, the Mexican-American border resembles

7. Thomas Barnett, 'The Pentagon's New Map', *Esquire*, March 2003: available from http://www.thurisa.org/newmap.htm; accessed August 14, 2003. See also: Thomas Barnett, 'Global Transaction Strategy', *Military Officer*, Vol. 1, No. 5, 2003 available at: http://www.nwc.navy.mil/newrulesets/GlobalTransactionStrategy.htm

8. 'Transnational Crime and Peacekeeping: Comparative Perspectives', *Cantigny Conference Report*, Sponsored by the McCormick-Tribune Foundation and organized by the Transnational Crime and Corruption Center, September 6–7, 2001, p. 14.

a war zone complete with barriers, armed soldiers, and now unmanned aerial vehicles (UAVs).

The last mega-trend is the overwhelming effect of the information explosion of the mass media. The effect of mass media, sometimes described as the "CNN effect" or the "CNN-drome," not only focuses national security officials on breaking crises, but it also creates media myths. One needs only to watch the famous Allianz commercial, which revolves around a father's promise to his little daughter. Real people possess a radically different life style than the "glitzy" world of this family. But this type of message causes some to question or, at worst, act. When the basic elements of human nature, especially greed, are combined with these four mega-trends unique to today's globalized world, sophisticated criminal activity runs rampant.

In the 21st century, international organized crime, from activities as simple as a stolen car ring criss-crossing the Adriatic or as sophisticated as the smuggling of components for weapons of mass destruction, has targeted countries in transition and must be viewed as a security threat. Activities of organized crime undermine the democratization process of many countries. This growing crisis of criminality attacks a nation an established democracy or one just emerging. It weakens the prosperity of its citizens and its economy; it undermines the citizens' trust in government and creates an atmosphere of cynicism; it tears down domestic security and, in extreme cases, the stability of an entire political system.[9]

Somalia, no longer a viable nation-state, but a failed state with no domestic security, has slipped into chaos because criminality under the cover of clan warfare is unbridled. Its capital, Mogadishu, has been divided among seven clan leaders and passage from one neighborhood to another can be dangerous, depending upon with whom one does business and how long one remains.[10] Somalia is a "basket case nation" beyond assistance. The chances of any regeneration of interest within the international community for this state or some kind of internal solution to Somalia's current plight are illusory.

---

9. 'Transnational Crime and Peacekeeping', p. 16.
10. 'Chaos Rules Somalia Decade After Battle,' *The Associated Press*, ABC NEWS.com; available from http://www.abcnews.go.com/wire/World/ap20031002_1759.html accessed October 14, 2003.

Another case study in growing criminality is Albania, which exacerbated the slide towards full-scale civil war in 1996–97. Domestic confidence in the Albanian government was severely shaken. Finally, a new post-Taliban Afghanistan economy will probably continue to depend on criminal activities, particularly its control of the market share of the global heroin production and export, which will exacerbate outside efforts to re-establish democratic governance in this conflict-torn region.

To understand the power of this growing crisis of organized criminality, the issue of trafficking must be set a context. If one could put a market value of global criminal goods and services, estimates would range from about $650 billion to $1 trillion; a vast amount of lost tax revenues.[11] At the Janes' Conference on Transnational Organized Crime (TOC) in September 2000, the figure $5 trillion was used without challenge from an audience full of experts. However, to place the enormous cost of criminal activity into a context whose order of magnitude lay people can comprehend, ask what the domestic drug problem cost a nation like Germany today? German taxpayers spend about 55,000 Euros to rehabilitate one drug addict.[12] However, just as individuals develop a drug addiction, nations are also at risk of becoming "hooked" on this traditional drug trade. Mexico's cartels alone yield $30 billion to $50 billion a year in hard currency from the United States, which is more than four times the revenue from oil, the country's leading legal export.[13]

This growing influence of drug money is the greatest single source of Mexican instability. The narcotics industry has worked its way into the fabric of Mexican society and is probably the country's largest employer. As in Colombia, drug dealers threaten to take control of the state. More worrying, senior Mexican officials—including those in charge of the antidrug effort—are routinely found to be working for drug cartels. Major drug traffickers have assembled their own private armies and operate without fear of prosecution. The

---

11. Mark Galeotti, 'Crimes of the new millennium', *Jane's Intelligence Review*, 01 August 2000, p. 1

12. Author's discussions with Dr. Guenther Beckstein, Bavarian Interior Minister, September 24, 1999.

13. Andrew Redding, 'Drug Money Runs the Latin Economy', Cleveland *Plain Dealer*, 17 October 1997, p. 1

control of Mexico by drug traffickers will be hard to reverse, especially given the central role the drug lords play in Mexican life and doing so might further destabilize the country.[14]

Drug trafficking has historically attracted international organized crime interest, but another form of trafficking is stealing market share; human trafficking or the commodication of persons has exploded. Our global community is witnessing the growth of a modern form of slavery. These modern traffickers treat men, women, children, and human organs as commodities to abuse, sell, and transport across borders like contraband cigarettes, illegal drugs, or stolen weapons. According to the United Nations, over one million people per year are sold into slavery. The globalization of our economies, a very high demand for personal services, a rise of unemployment (especially among women), the spiraling need for organ transplants and the Internet, all facilitate the rapid, unregulated enticement and movement of human capital. The dark side of the Internet involves fraud, theft, and pervasive pornography, as well as criminal organizations intent upon exploitation of humans.

Human trafficking is a highly attractive business because it is low cost and low risk but promises high, non-taxable financial gains. The United Nations' Interregional Crime Research Institute previously estimated that human trafficking alone generated over $7 billion per year in trade. Only two years later, the United Nations Children's Fund (UNICEF) reported that the 1.2 million children were trafficked and generated $10 billion per year.[15] Human smuggling is the fastest growing criminal business in the world, according to Under-Secretary-General Pino Arlacchi, the head of the United Nations Office for Drug Control and Crime Prevention.[16]

This humanitarian crisis has become so acute that President Bush commented upon its nature, size, and effects in his United Nations General Assembly address on September 23, 2003:

---

14. Steven R. David, "Breaking Mexico's Habit," *Foreign Affairs*, January 1999/ February 1999, p. 103

15. Jeremy Lovell, 'One Million Children Trafficked Each Year,' ABCNEWS.com. July 2, 2003.

16. Zoran Kusovac, 'People Trafficking: Europe's New Problem,' *Jane's Intelligence Review*, September 1, 2000. p. 1.

> 'There is a special evil in the abuse and exploitation of the most innocent and vulnerable. The victims of sex trade see little of life before they see the very worst of life, an underworld of brutality and lonely fear.'[17]

Although images of ships barely able to stay afloat and weighed down with illegal immigrants are beginning to focus world attention on the question of illegal immigration, human trafficking is increasing dramatically while remaining hidden from view.

Most illegal entries or human trafficking into the European Union (EU) follows land routes and has become a daily occurrence for the eastern-most members of the EU—Germany, Austria, and Italy, and the only member state not within the contiguous EU area, Greece. The majority of the "illegals" who successfully enter the EU without work permits originate from either from Eastern Europe or Asia. Eastern Europeans compose two distinct groups. The first group is made up of citizens from the former Soviet republics, mostly Ukraine, with Russia trailing far behind. Statistics indicate the greatest number of illegal immigrants among the Asian groups come from Turkey.

Interestingly, the main obstacle to examining trafficking today is that a reasonably precise estimate of the problem is unavailable and can only be projected from the numbers of illegals who fail to reach their final destination.[18] The German Bundeskriminalamt (BKA) developed an analysis of the prostitution patterns from data gathered in 2001. Among the 200,000 prostitutes known to be working in Germany, 69% percent came from Eastern Europe: 14.2% from Belarus, 13.0% from Ukraine, 12.1% from Lithuania, 8.5 from Poland, and, 4.1% from Latvia. The remaining 30% percent came from Asia and Africa. Over 50% percent of these women were between 18 and 24 years old.[19] A criminal organization can earn between $120,000 and $150,000 from a woman forced into prostitution.[20] In the words of one Mafia boss: 'The earnings are incredible.

---

17. George W. Bush, 'Transcript of Bush U.N. Address,' CNN.com, 24 September 2003.
18. Kusovac, p. 1.
19. 'Verkauft wie eine Kuh (Sold Like a Cow).' *Der Spiegel*, Number 26, Juni 23, 2003, p. 46.
20. *Cantigny Conference Report*, p. 14.

The overhead is low; you don't have to buy cars and guns. Drugs you sell once and they are gone. Women can earn money for a long time.'[21]

Trafficking activity alone generates incredible capital for the criminal networks that exploit this trade. The real economic extent of fees charged to facilitate illegal immigration can only be estimated and the means of analysis are admittedly rather unsophisticated. Based upon a $2,500 rough estimate per head per passage (costs reported vary from $1,000 for passage from Romania to $15,000 from Iran) and using the figure of over 40,000 illegal immigrants caught entering Austria alone in 1999, the market share would be a staggering $100 million, just for the recorded cases for one year for one country alone.[22] Exact profit figures are only realized following an arrest. *Operation Twister* recently caught a Czech-German gang that had smuggled about 400 Chinese and Vietnamese recruited for menial labor in Chinese restaurants throughout Germany. The gang earned nearly $400,000 in 2002.[23]

Unfortunately, this flood will continue because no disincentives exist. Arrest only leads to a minor infraction rather than a serious criminal penalty; payments are made prior to the transit with no obligation to the client in case the operation is not a success; and illegal immigrants demonstrate a high degree of determination to get into the EU. 'Your wares come to you without any need to search or advertise, they stick to a code of silence and if you get caught, the evidence against you tries to run away.'[24] They keep coming back until they are successful.

During an interagency border security operation in the United States that spanned several months and focused exclusively on one point of entry, a rail yard, several illegals were apprehended, arrested, and deported only to return in a matter of weeks.[25] Even a sleepy little town

21. Quote provided in a discussion with a German serving BKA officer. The fate of these women is horrific and provides another critical subject for further analysis and discussion.

22. Kusovac, p. 2.

23. 'Gang of human smugglers busted', *Expatica, News and Community for the Expatriate* available from http://www.expatia.com/source/site_article.asp? accessed on March 8, 2004.

24. Kusovac, p. 2.

25. The author was responsible for the coordination of this inter-agency operation in 1988.

in Bavaria, Garmisch-Partenkirchen, has become a choke point in the illegal trafficking pipe line because it sits at the bifurcation of two highways entering from Austria. In February 2004, a busload of Chinese was stopped at a border police random check point and illegals were seized by the police and deported. These checks are by law random and very infrequent. One can only surmise real flow through this choke point.[26]

Strenuous research of trafficking is not necessary in order to draw conclusions about the scale and pervasiveness of this problem in Europe: it is a highly visible phenomenon. Within Europe, for example, on a drive down the coast from Rome to Naples or from Prague to the German border, one cannot help but notice prostitutes seemingly picketed in near military precision approximately every kilometer by warming barrels to ward off the night chill. In the Czech Republic, prostitution by trafficked women working to feign entry into the EU is largely concentrated near the country's borders with Austria to the south, Germany to the west and north, and to a lesser degree, with Poland to the northeast. The infamous stretch of highway E55 on northern Bohemia's Czech-German border, especially the small town of Dubi, is known for the prostitutes lining its roads. Many of the prostitutes not only rely on their jobs as their main source of income to finance their expenditures, but also, must support the people who control them. It is not uncommon for these women to pay up to 80% of their earnings to pimps and other middlemen. In clubs, their profits are often reduced by half, with bogus fines being levied by club owners at every opportunity. Police allegedly turn a blind eye to these activities and most prostitutes are hesitant to be identified when pointing to instances of corruption. Unfortunately for these unprotected women, whether in a major city or the border regions, prostitutes communicate the same stories: they observe police officers regularly on the take.[27]

However, women are not the only victims of this wholesale trafficking horror. Facilitated by the Internet, the sexual exploitation of children is rapidly becoming a mass global industry as well. From sleazy brothels in back alleys to online stalkers, over 1 million children

26. *Kreis Bote*, Wochenend-Journal, Nr. 07-GAP-13./14. February 2004, p. 1.

27. Kazi Stastna, 'Taxing the Professional', *Central European Review*, Vol. 1, No. 22, November 1999, p. 6.

are being sexually victimized worldwide.[28] This clandestine market includes human trafficking, sex tourism, child prostitution, and all forms of pornography. It is fed by poverty, discrimination, weak legislation, poor education, organized crime gangs and, tragically, a seemingly insatiable perverted sexual demand, and law enforcement agencies cannot cope with the extent and global nature of the problem. According to June Kane, communications advisor to the Second World Congress against Commercial Sexual Exploitation of Children, advances in technology and trafficking are posing serious new threats to the fight against the commercial sexual exploitation of children. She emphasized that mobile phones and text messaging technology, among others, have become tools of the trade and that web sites are use to provide real-time, online images of exploited children at customers' requests.[29]

The most gruesome and dehumanizing aspect of human trafficking involves the trafficking of human body parts. Based in the former Soviet Union, an international "transplant" Mafia is capitalizing on a global organ shortage crisis by trafficking live donors into recipient states to sell their lungs and kidneys. The United States and Israel provide the primary target markets. Using false student or tourist visas, some form of fraudulent documentation, illicit organ donors from Moldova, the poorest state carved from the former Soviet Union, enter the United States, often at John F. Kennedy Airport. They are spirited to local hospitals, where their organs are removed and sold. The Moldovan connection, the first international organized crime organ trafficking ring uncovered in the United States, takes advantage of the huge global demand for lifesaving organs and the acute scarcity of supply.

To illustrate this supply and demand crisis, in the US, about 86,000 peoples are currently waiting for transplants. Last year approximately 6,000 people or about 17 a day, died for want of an organ. In some cases, Moldavian donors have duped doctors into believing they are giving their organs altruistically to family members. However, there are clearly doctors who knowingly profit from it. Some beneficiaries of this nauseating criminal activity are believed to be children,

28. Lovell, p. 1.

29. 'Child Sex Exploitation Forum to Focus on IT, Trafficking', Child Labor News Service, December 15, 2001, available from http://www.globalmarch.org/clns/clns-15-12-2001.html accessed on October 17, 2003.

whose wealthy parents pay huge sums to save their child's life. Nevertheless, impoverished Moldavians are in a lose-lose situation. They find themselves in this dilemma because they owe the mafia money. If the debtor "sells" an organ, the mafia offers to forgive the debt. The hapless Moldovan returns home at once debt- and organ-free.[30]

University of California anthropologist Nancy Scheper-Hughes, who has tracked organ profiteers in Latin America, Central Asia and Russia noted that: '...some of these outlaw transplant operations are 'cloak and dagger,' others operate in the gray nether world of loopholes and soft corruptions of waiting lists for tightly regulated and rationed organs.'[31]

For the organ recipient, the blight of endemic poverty found primarily in Barnett's "Non-Integrating Gap," can make the cost of an ill-gotten kidney much less than regular treatment on a dialysis machine. So many poor villagers in India sell their kidneys, India has become known as the "kidney belt." A Madras slum is widely known as "Kidney-vakkam" because organ sales play a large role in the local economy. India recently banned the organ trade, but that has not prevented an entrenched class of organ brokers from continuing operations on the black market (visitors to Villivakkam can still see women with large, curving scars visible under their sari tops). The black-market nature of such sales makes market cost of these organs difficult to determine, but young women go under the knife in exchange for dowry money—about $20,000 with the organ broker's take between $1,000 and $5,000.[32]

However, India and Moldova are not the only "organ markets" in the world. Police in Ryazan, a Russian city about an hour's drive south of Moscow, discovered a grandmother allegedly trying to sell her 5-year-old grandson, asking $90,000 for his organs.[33] Further south

30. This story was widely reported and an American intelligence officer serving in the region confirmed the information to the author.

31. Harry Kreisler, Interview with Dr. Nancy Scheper-Hughes, 'Habits of a Militant Anthropologist-Conversation', *Conversations with History*: Institute of International Studies, UC Berkeley, 14 December 1999.

32. Sanjay Kumar, 'Despite Ban, Organs Still Sold in India,' Reuters Health, March 9, 2001 pp. 1–2. Also available http://userwww.service.emory.edu/uskrause/wp/pr-rubin.doc

33. 'Russian Grandmother 'wanted to sell child for organs." CNN.com. posted 1:14 PM EST, November 28, 2000.

in the Caucasus, security officers recently solicited prisoners condemned to death in Azerbaijan for their hearts in order to provide one to their ailing President Aliyev, who has been awaiting a heart transplant in the United States.[34] The desparate desire for even the most basic of commodities, a television, has tempted some impoverished Eastern Europeans attempting to evolve into homo connectus to even sell their children.[35] The desperate need for organs, the miracles of modern surgery, and the total immorality of the criminal element, create strange bedfellows in our globalized world.

Human trafficking creates profits that in turn criminalize the banking system; notable scandals have occurred in Switzerland and Liechtenstein. David Chaikin, a noted Australian lawyer and anti-money laundering expert who had worked with the Australian Federal Attorney General's Department as senior assistant secretary, noted: "The danger and jurisdictional reach of the Russian Mafia cannot be underestimated."[36]

In 1999, the German external intelligence service, the Bundesnachrichdienst (BND), compiled a report for the German government chronicling the activities of the "Organisatzya" in the former Soviet Union and confirming this sale of children's body organs.[37] As a result, the guarding of a state's border from illegal trafficking has become more dangerous. Switzerland with its 1900 kilometers of frontier to secure, 48 attacks on border guards were reported in 2003, and these included drive-by shootings and the murder of guards' dependents.[38]

People ensnared in the web cast by human traffickers are not the only victims. The nation state can develop a criminal connection to state corruption: Official political power fuses with professional criminal power and democracies and governability are weakened. Alliances that enhance the interests of those who wield political power with those

34. Author's discussion with a US intelligence officer who is serving in the region, September 21, 2003.

35. Nicholas Wood, 'For Albanians, It's Come to This: A Son for a TV' *New York Times*, 13 November 2003.

36. Donna S. Cueto, 'Macapagal urged to bring case to Swiss President', *The Nation*, Posted: 1:18 AM Manila time, May 19, 2002. pp. 1–4.

37. Allan Hall, "Russian Mafia Kills Children for Transplants," *Scotland on Sunday*, 14 November 1999, p. 21.

38. 'Border guards risk new dangers', *Neue Zürcher Zeitung*. NZZ Online, September 30, 2003, posted at 16:15, Swissinfo.

who, by their occupation, reject the rule of law, threaten real national security. In the contemporary debate on corruption dominated by groups such as Transparency International, the role of international organized crime is given little attention. Their annual rankings of state fraudulence that treat corruption as a condition that can be resolved through peer pressure, transparency, and efforts to establish good governance fail to recognize the real essence of the problem.

As Phil Williams has noted: 'From an organized crime perspective, however, corruption is not so much a condition as an instrument. The major question from this perspective concerns who is corrupting whom for what purposes, and by what means. Organized crime uses instrumental, or targeted corruption, as a major instrument of influence. Its efforts can range from operational corruption, designed to facilitate its illegal activities, to systemic corruption that not only reduces a state's defenses, but seeks to transform attitudes and policies towards organized crime from hostility to acquiescence or even collusion.'[39] He added: "There is no better 'front' for organized crime intent on trafficking than a state."[40]

## CONCLUSIONS

All states Europe and Eurasia contain some political-criminal nexus. In nations where the political-criminal nexus is strong, one finds pervasive corruption in both the judiciary and within local law enforcement agencies, creating a protected criminal element along with their political collaborators. Every day citizens are denied justice, which further undermines public trust in the rule of law and democratic governance. The process of democratization can be stalled or even reversed if the connection between politics, business, crime and corruption becomes dominant. At worse, this can precipitate state failure and collapse. While trafficking of any sort—drugs, humans, or organs—has a profound impact on societal and

39. Phil Williams, 'Crime and corruption: the role of state collusion', *Jane's Intelligence Review*, 23 August 2000, p. 1.

40. Remarks by Phil Williams, Director of the Matthew B. Ridgeway Center for International Security Studies, International Affairs and Urban Affairs, at the University of Pittsburgh, at Janes' Conference on Transnational Organized Crime (TOC) 19–21 September 2000.

economic security, it can also lead to the hollowing out of the state or region, the emergence of a state-criminal complex that has the ability to undermine the legitimacy and stability of a state, whether it be democratic or authoritarian.

One might ask whether trafficking and its supporting international organized crime networks are in every sense a force for instability? Might it not be argued that sophisticated, adaptable, and efficient organized criminal groups might actually provide regions with services in the faced of the collapse of the center, if only to increase their legitimacy within society? Could a nation-state live and develop in symbiosis with them, integrating criminal elites into society and the white economy as the criminal elites gradually indicate their willingness to legitimize their operations and enter the mainstream? Although such sentiments have superficial allure, such a process can only take place alongside the acceptance that substantial criminal elements will still practice the so-called "Vampire Syndrome," and that the clandestine nature of influence does not concern or affect its citizenry; or if blackmail and political corruption are just another form of tax; or if illegal power cliques are just another form of a political party.

Claire Sterling popularized the notion of a "Pax Mafiosa," in which international organized crime syndicates worked together efficiently and harmoniously, and divided the globe among them. There is ample evidence of this cooperation. The Sicilian Mafia or Cosa Nostra, the Neapolitan Camorra, the Calabrian Ndrangheta, and the Sacra Corona Unita send "ambassadors" to Albanian drug families to facilitate the orderly trafficking of humans and drugs.[41] International criminal organizations are targeting new democracies with free markets. This "cooperative criminality" does create threats for the nation-state and for regional and international law enforcement agencies: cooperative co-existence is a myth.

In the face of this soft security threat, how might states and agencies respond? Globalization, which has helped create the problem through its functions as an accelerator, a magnifier, and an amplifier, should also contribute to the solution. While globalization accelerates the contacts between criminal organizations and illicit

41. Comments made by the Chief, Strategic Analysis, of the Italian SISDE at the 3rd Annual Conference of the U.S. Office of Personnel Management: The World-wide War on Terrorism-'Countering the Threat' Chief, on May 12, 2003.

actors, it can also help to enable, accelerate, and spread a network contacts and connections among actors trying to combat international organized crime. Globalization should function to unite diverse actors.[42] Networks can be used to fight networks. The two approaches that follow require astute networking.

The first approach is regulatory: States must not only enhance their law enforcement and judicial capabilities, but also coordinate individual responses with other national, regional, and global enforcement bodies and criminal justice systems. In addition to emphasis on enforcement cooperation, education must be provided. Nation-states must not attempt to hide criminal activity from its citizens who see the problem daily, but illuminate the problem of trafficking. Trafficking must be deglamorized. The final approach is non-regulatory. Government and private sector cooperation must build a strong societal and cultural foundation in order to strengthen the legitimacy of legal system and protected legal norms and standards. The Sicilian question: "Who do you belong to?" must be replaced by the development of a deeper "culture of lawfulness," policy makers and law enforcement agencies must develop allies in different cultural strata: from all religious communities, from the arts, from the entertainment world and from education.

Leoluca Orlando, Mayor of Palermo (a former hotbed of Mafia violence) argued that the regulatory and non- regulatory approaches must function like the wheels of a cart.[43] To ensure success, to stay on course and to make progress, the cart's wheels must be synchronized. Increased contacts and connections throughout the spectrum of actors trying to combat international organized crime—networks fighting networks—will make this synchronization possible and diminish the reach of organized crime: "As crime crosses all borders, so must law enforcement. If the rule of law is undermined not only in one country but in many, then those who defend it cannot limit themselves only to national means."[44]

42. Cantigny Conference Report, p. 8.

43. Remarks made by Leoluca Orlando, Mayor of Palermo, Italy on September 17, 1999, to the Marshall Center's Senior Executive Seminar, SES 99–5.

44. Kofi Annan, 'The Convention Against Transnational Organized Crime', Palermo, Italy, December 12, 2000.

# WEAPONS TRANSFERS AS A SOFT SECURITY ISSUE IN EASTERN EUROPE: LEGAL AND ILLICIT ASPECTS

LEONID RYABIKHIN AND JEVGENIA VIKTOROVA

## INTRODUCTION: ARMS TRANSFERS AS A (SOFT) SECURITY THREAT

Generally, the topic of weapons transfers is associated with hard, or military, security. However, there are certain ways in which it also pertains to soft security concerns. Through the civilian "connection" of defense industries, weapons transfers acquire significance for the economic and social stability in the producing and exporting countries.[1] For the receiving states, weapons can have a dual effect of

1. See, for example, Ian Anthony, 'Introduction', pp. 1–15 in Ian Anthony (ed.), *Russia and the Arms Trade* (SIPRI/Oxford University Press, 1998), p. 2; or Terrence R. Guay, *At Arm's Length: The European Union and Europe's Defence Industry* (Houndmills et al.: Macmillan, 1998).

strengthening the state—which is often a concern of weak governments in the developing world—or, to the contrary, further aggravating internal instability through the diversion of weapons into the hands of insurgencies, paramilitaries, criminal organizations, or other unsavory non-state actors thriving on conflict. These ambivalent effects are often associated with the distinction made in arms proliferation literature between major conventional weapons (which require significant technical skills to operate and a certain legitimacy to acquire, as they are bulkier and transactions are more difficult to conceal) which ultimately enhance the stability of governments,[2] and, on the other hand, small arms and light weapons, which are produced by a far greater number of manufacturers and can be procured through a variety of licit and illicit channels, being cheaper, less conspicuous and more difficult to trace, as well as easily transportable and manageable even by untrained soldiers, including children.[3]

The trade in both conventional and light weapons can involve uneasy compromises between the objectives of enhancing state security (assessed through the magnitude of weapons stocks) and its internal stability (achieved in the longer run by investing in economic development),[4] and both thus have soft security implications. However, the threat is perhaps more difficult to counter in the latter case, as uncontrolled proliferation of the "tools of violence"[5] can cancel the determination of governments to pursue the policies of development rather than forceful pacification of their countries.

2. William J. Durch, *Constructing Regional Security: The Role of Arms Transfers, Arms Control, and Reassurance* (Houndmills et al.: Palgrave, 2000).
3. Keith Krause, *Small Arms and Light Weapons: Proliferation Processes and Policy Options* (International Security Research and Outreach Programme, International Security Bureau, July 2000, at http://www.smallarmssurvey.org/AddRes/krause_proliferation.PDF), p. v, accessed 4 April 2003.
4. cf. Mark Duffield, *Global Governance and the New Wars* (London and New York: Zed Books, 2002); *Controlling the Availability and Unlawful Use of Arms at the International Level: the United Nations and Civil Society* (http://www.nisat.org/default.asp?page=publications/pub_videos.htm 1998), accessed 10 September 2003.
5. Ed J. Laurance, 'Controlling the availability and unlawful use of arms at the international level: The United Nations and civil society', in *Controlling the Availability and Unlawful Use of Arms at the International Level: the United Nations and Civil Society* (http://www.nisat.org/default.asp?page=publications/pub_videos.htm, 1998), accessed 10 September 2003.

To a great extent (cases of superpower asymmetric military engagement apart), small arms represent the level at which contemporary (post-Cold War) wars are fought. Out of the more than 50 major conflicts that have broken out since 1990, light weapons were the only arms used in 46; only a few conflicts (the 1991 Gulf War, air strikes against Serbia, the antiterrorism war in Afghanistan, and the recent allied campaign in Iraq) were dominated by heavy weapons.[6] Analysts have noted a mutual connection between the availability of small arms that fuel armed conflict, and the fluid politico-economic situation created by violence, which is exploited to make profit from arms deals in war zones[7]—a phenomenon known as the "economies of war."[8] While it may be arguable whether the availability of weapons as such increases propensity to violence,[9] the accumulation of arms in the hands of hostile social or ethnic groups creates dynamics reminiscent of the classical security dilemma, increasing insecurity and mistrust.[10] It also prolongs conflicts and increases civilian casualties where violent conflict has already broken out.

Another way in which soft and hard aspects of security are intertwined with regard to armaments is their use. Weapons used in peacekeeping operations are rarely meant to be used against the conflicting parties or directly to deter insurgent violence (sometimes not even for self-defense of the peacekeepers or aid workers),[11] but to symbolically increase the credibility of the peace effort,[12] providing a sense of security and order for implementing a range of disarmament and development policies carried out by the UN, International NGOs and other members of the "strategic complexes of liberal

6. See *1996 SIPRI Yearbook* (Stockholm: SIPRI, 1996).

7. Laurance, op. cit.

8. Carolyn Nordstrom, 'Contested Identities/Essentially Contested Powers', pp. 93–115 in Kumar Rupesinghe (ed.), *Conflict Transformation* (Basingstoke: Macmillan, 1995).

9. The Rwandan case, where most killlings were done with machetes, is often cited to counterweigh this claim.

10. cf. Peter Herby, 'Developing a Humanitarian Law Approach to the Problem of Arms Availability', in *Controlling the Availability and Unlawful Use of Arms at the International Level: the United Nations and Civil Society* (http://www.nisat.org/default.asp?page=publications/pub_videos.htm, 1998), accessed 10 September 2003.

11. cf. William Shawcross, *Deliver Us from Evil* (London, Bloomsbury, 1999); Michael Ignatieff, *The Warrior's Honour* (London, Vintage, 1999).

12. Joseba Zulaika and William A. Douglass, *Terror and Taboo: The Follies, Fables, and Faces of Terrorism* (New York & London: Routledge 1996), pp. 84–86.

peace,"[13] thus contributing to the "softening" of the local security agenda.

As a contrary motion, a soft approach to the problem of proliferation is gaining greater prominence.[14] Despite certain recent attempts at military solutions to the threat of nuclear proliferation sought by the US and their allies in the Middle East (which may of course be one of the ways of dealing with weapons developed locally, and not shipped to the unstable regions from First and Second World producers or brokers), there is a notable trend towards controlling weapons supplies through negotiated solutions such as harmonisation of export policies of the producers ("codes of conduct"), or sets of restrictive measures on destinations such as end-user certificates for weapons, equipment, and their components and spare parts.[15]

## REGIONAL DYNAMICS OF ARMS TRADE: LEGAL TRANSFERS

Amidst global concerns about proliferation of weapons of mass destruction and arms supplies to the regions of devastating internal conflict, Europe as a whole looks relatively unproblematic (perhaps with the exceptions of the Balkans and Caucasus), compared to the bulk of the developing world.[16] Although it is important to note the global reach of proliferation routes, for most countries it is their immediate regional environment that determines their security concerns, including those stemming from weapons transfers.[17] Accordingly, different regions will have their own specific dynamics of arms production and trade, arising both from their global roles and local opportunities and pressures.

13. Duffield, op. cit.
14. See Sergei Kortunov, 'The Influence of External Factors on Russia's Arms Export Policy', pp. 93–106 in Ian Anthony (ed.), *Russia and the Arms Trade* (SIPRI/Oxford University Press, 1998), pp. 98–99.
15. Durch, op.cit., pp. 17–18.
16. Durch (ibid.) delimits the developing world as comprising Africa, Central and South America, Asia apart from China and Japan, the Pacific except Australia and New Zealand, the countries of the former Soviet Union, and the Middle East.
17. cf. Durch, op. cit., p. 61.

Since the end of the Cold War, politics in Europe have been defined by the perceived absence of military threat—although during the 1990s Russia occasionally voiced its concerns regarding NATO's eastward enlargement as undermining (military) multipolarity, and more recently, the anxiety about the superpower nuclear confrontation has resurfaced in the form of heightened awareness of the destructiveness of international (weapons of mass destruction, WMD) terrorism.[18] In this light, greater attention is being paid to the problem of illicit movement of weapons that end up in the hands of non-state actors, either through covert trade or diversion from the properly sanctioned supplies to politically unstable regions (described as, for example, "destabilizing accumulations").[19] In accord with this differentiation, the remainder of this section will cover the problems of legal transfers, while the following section will address the threat of illicit and illegal proliferation of weapons in the region.

Legal transfers account for 80–90% of the global arms transfers, the rest being shared between illicit grey market transfers (when governments or their agents exploit loopholes or circumvent national and/or international laws and policies) and illegal black market transfers (which take place in clear violation of national and/or international laws and without official government consent or control, although they may involve corrupt government officials acting on their own for personal gain).[20] The majority of illegal transfers involve small arms and light weapons,[21] with up to 25% of trade in them being conducted illegally.[22]

Keith Krause referred to legal and licit transfers as the "primary circuit" of weapons proliferation, which, although being authorised by the governments of both exporting and importing countries, may still represent a threat in terms of upsetting regional balances of military power.[23] They also serve as a starting point for nearly all subsequent

---

18. See e.g. Charles W. Kegley, Jr. (ed.), *The New Global Terrorism: Characteristics, Causes, Controls* (Upper Saddle River, NJ: Prentice Hall, 2003).
19. See Wassenaar Arrangement homepage (www.wassenaar.org/list/wa-list...), accessed 26 September 2003.
20. *Small Arms Survey: Profiling the Problem* (Oxford: Oxford University Press, 2001), pp. 141–166.
21. See Krause, 'Small Arms and Light Weapons', p. v.
22. *The Economist*, 16 May 1998, p. 47.
23. Krause, 'Small Arms and Light Weapons', pp. v–vi.

diversions into the "secondary circuit" of proliferation concerning illicit and illegal deals: "*Virtually all illicit weapons transferred were, at some point in their life, legally produced or procured.*"[24]

From either the legal or illegal transfers perspective, Europe is by no means internally homogenous, with significant differences existing between the West and the East, as well as within these broadly defined regions. The imperatives of adjusting to the post-Cold War conditions for arms trade and production[25] have yielded different responses from the countries of the region. In addition, their policy orientations are continually shaped by the general European and Transatlantic developments, the main trends being set by the EU and NATO eastward enlargements and the accompanying internal reform of these organisations. Altering the terms of regional politico-economic relations, these processes affect both the acceding states and those left outside the present rounds of enlargement or even lists of candidate countries.

On the part of the new NATO members, two related concerns are often voiced: one about upgrading their military equipment and armaments in order to meet alliance standards, and the other about the surplus stocks of weapons and ammunition that will or have become outdated by NATO membership. As the central and eastern European (CEE) and Former Soviet Union countries differ in terms of magnitude of their defense industries inherited from Warsaw Treaty (WTO)/USSR times, weapons stocks, the size of the armed forces and territory, as well as defense "ambitions" (such as self-reliance in defense matters), the task of adjusting to NATO requirements has different features in each individual case.

For countries with modest or no defense industries, like Estonia, the upgrading of armaments inevitably concerns the import of new weapons and equipment, coupled with disposal or modernization of the old stocks. For those with significant capacities in defence industries (such as Poland or Czech Republic), the challenge is complemented by the necessity of maintaining their profitability while—in the case

24. Krause, 'Small Arms and Light Weapons', p. vi, emphasis in original.
25. See, e.g., Ian Anthony, 'Trends in Post-Cold War International Arms Transfers', pp. 16–37 in Ian Anthony (ed.), *Russia and the Arms Trade* (SIPRI/Oxford University Press, 1998).

of new NATO members and candidates—reconfiguring the production along NATO-compatible lines.

Since government procurement usually engages only part of the defense plants' production capacity, economic imperatives make export of weapons the second best option.[26] Governments may play different roles in determining export policies, from issuing export licenses to negotiating and subsidising arms sales abroad; privatized or not, defense companies remain in the sphere of close attention from the state.[27]

However, the symbiosis of politics and economics has at different times been undermined by imbalances towards one or the other. Ian Anthony maintained that the arms producing countries of Central and Eastern Europe (including Russia and Ukraine) have yet to strike a balance between foreign policy, strategic and economic considerations in determining priority directions in arms production and trade policies and the corresponding arms export control legislation.[28] As an example, Russian liberalization of arms exports in the beginning of the 1990s, instead of compensating for the post-Cold War losses in the share of the weapons market, has further undermined the defense industry's economic viability because of the unchecked competition among the producers that brought prices down below the manufacturing costs.[29] Perpetual institutional restructuring of the Russian state agencies in charge of arms exports, coupled with the lack of clarity regarding the prospects of military reform, had added to the producers' confusion.[30] Needless to say, stable relations between the Russian arms producers and export (control) agencies contribute

26. See Irina Korobinskaya and Peter Litavrin, 'Military-Technical Cooperation Between Russia and Countries of East-Central Europe, pp. 177–193 in Ian Anthony (ed.), *Russia and the Arms Trade* (SIPRI/Oxford University Press, 1998).

27. Ibid.; cf. Richard A. Bitzinger, *Towards a Brave New Arms Industry?* (IISS, Adelphi Paper 356, 2003).

28. Anthony, op. cit., 'Introduction', pp. 8–9.

29. Ian Anthony, 'Economic Dimensions of Soviet and Russian Arms Exports', pp. 71–92 in Ian Anthony (ed.), *Russia and the Arms Trade* (SIPRI/Oxford University Press, 1998); and Kortunov, op. cit.

30. Anthony, ibid.; Peter Litavrin, 'The Process of Policy Making and Licensing for Conventional Arms Transfers', pp. 107–116; Yuriy Kirshin, 'The Role of the Ministry of Defence in the Export of Conventional Weapons', pp. 117–123; and Elena Denezhkina, 'Russian Defence Firms and the External Market', pp. 124–145 in Ian Anthony (ed.), *Russia and the Arms Trade* (SIPRI/Oxford University Press, 1998).

to the general improvement of regional security in Europe and adjacent areas, by reducing incentives to pursue illegal avenues for arms trade.

As the East-Central European importers' share of total Russian arms exports is below ten percent,[31] this cooperation may have more political than economic significance. Maintaining links with the new and future NATO members will contribute to Russia's closer relations with the alliance. Although for many CEE states (such as Hungary) replacing aging Russian weaponry with Western models, their higher cost notwithstanding, has become something of a political imperative,[32] analysts note that NATO membership is no reason for discarding the Russian-produced equipment, as long as it is compatible with the weapons systems used by the alliance (Germany, for instance, made good use of the MIG-29 aircraft inherited from DDR stocks).[33] Thus, Bulgaria and Slovakia enjoy continuing military supplies from Russia, with Poland occupying something of a middle ground in this regard.[34] At the same time, the links between the old and new NATO members are likewise strengthened by arms transfers; as an example, Canada, Denmark, Finland, Germany, Norway, Sweden, the UK, and the US dominate the list of source countries for the bulk of weapons, equipment, and ammunition received by Estonia during 1993–2003.[35]

EU enlargement will likewise carry with it the requirement of compatibility—although this mostly concerns legislation regulating the arms trade. The challenges faced are two-fold: first, bringing the accession states' legal acts into correspondence with EU standards, and, second, harmonizing the internal EU legislation on arms transfers. The 1997 Programme for Preventing and Combating Illicit Trafficking in Conventional Arms, the 1998 Code of Conduct on Arms Exports (signed up to by the candidate countries), and the 1999 Joint

31. See Anthony, 'Economic Dimensions of Soviet and Russian Arms Exports', p. 77; Litavrin, op.cit., p. 112; Korobinskaya and Litavrin, op. cit., p. 183.
32. Korobinskaya and Litavrin, op. cit., p. 190.
33. Ibid., p. 184.
34. Ibid., pp. 185–192.
35. Data obtained from the Norwegian Initiative on Small Arms Transfers (www.nisat.org); US Arms Transfers Database Search, Arms Sales Monitoring Project (www.fas.org.asmp/profiles/sales_db.htm); Estonia's Ministry of Defence web site (http://mod.gov.ee), accessed on 3 April 2003.

Action on Small Arms,[36] if not without drawbacks, manifest significant progress in the second challenge.

Still, all these initiatives bear signs of an eternal tension between the supranational "good faith" fostering closer foreign policy and defence integration, and the traditional commitment to the national interest (manifested, for instance, in the reluctance to part with the provisions of Article 223 of the Treaty of Rome, which leaves matters of the defense industry to the sole discretion of member states).[37] This tension is also discernible among the countries joining the European Union, who feel that too much defense cooperation within the EU would undermine their newly established Transatlantic links and reduce US support for the East-European dimension of NATO.[38] In this light, it is doubtful that in the near future, European defense firms will endeavor cooperation beyond the by now habitual projects of joint weapons production on the principle of *juste retour* (such as the development of the Eurofighter), which are politically, if not economically, justifiable to the national constituencies.[39]

Within Europe, the general trend has been one of reduction in military expenditure, which increases the pressure on the arms producing countries to export—a task increasingly difficult due to similar tendencies in the rest of the world (with the exceptions of Latin America, where the levels of spending have remained relatively stable, and Asia, where military expenditure has increased in the last decade).[40]

Changing also is the character of arms deals, as countries eager to develop their own defense industries, for example, Turkey, increasingly opt for various forms of industrial cooperation (from co-production to technology transfers) rather than purchasing finished

---

36. *Small Arms Survey* (2001), pp. 270–271.

37. See Durch, op. cit.; Paul Cornish, *Arms Trade and Europe* (London: Royal Institute of International Affairs, 1995); Guay, op. cit., pp. 48–49; Ian Davis, *The Regulation of Arms and Dual-Use Exports: Germany, Sweden and the UK* (Oxford: SIPRI/Oxford University Press, 2002).

38. Prime Minister Juhan Parts, 'Peaministri ettekanne Euroopa Liidu põhiseadusliku lepingu projektist Riigikogus 25.09' (PM's Speech on EU Constitution Project at the Estonian Parliament) (25 September 2003, at http://www.riik.ee/z2/avalik/file?id=7281).

39. Guay, op. cit., pp. 40–71.

40. Anthony, 'Trends in Post-Cold War International Arms Transfers', pp. 24–26.

products.[41] With a growing share of transfers in the form of offsets, cooperation in defense matters is likely to "soften," with economic considerations driving its agenda alongside the more traditional military concerns. Just how far-reaching will be the spillover effects in terms of soft security remains to be observed in the relations between the European weapons-producing states and the importing countries of other regions.

## ILLICIT AND ILLEGAL WEAPONS TRANSFERS

Legal transfers can be diverted into illegal paths in a number of ways. While some of them (such as direct government sponsorship of arms to non-state actors, violations of arms embargoes, or end-user undertakings) refer to both major conventional weapons and small arms, others (theft from government stocks, army and law enforcement units, gun shops, and private citizens; or the ant trade—the smuggling of legally bought arms into another country in small increments) rather "suit" small arms and light weapons.[42] Krause's "secondary circuit" of arms proliferation includes all transactions that are unauthorized by governments or conducted covertly, from the domestic "leakage" of legally held arsenals in both producer and recipient states (theft, loss, illicit transfers) to acquisitions by non-state actors (insurgent groups, organized crime, private security forces, private dealers, individuals) within or across state borders, to weapons retransfers between non-state actors.[43] Being particularly susceptible to trafficking, small arms and light weapons will be our primary concern in this section.

Unsurprisingly, obtaining data on illicit transfers is prone to certain difficulties, due to the very covert character of this activity. While information on the known facts of illicit and illegal transfers is scant and unreliable, it is equally difficult to disprove unfounded allegations which can easily become "common knowledge."[44] Curiously,

41. Ibid., p. 26.

42. *Small Arms Survey* (2002, at http://www.smallarmssurvey.org/Yearbook/EngPRkitCH3_11.06.02.pdf).

43. Krause, 'Small Arms and Light Weapons', p. vi.

44. cf. Ian Anthony, 'Illicit Arms Transfers', pp. 217–232 in Ian Anthony (ed.), *Russia and the Arms Trade* (Oxford: SIPRI/Oxford University Press, 1998).

reliable statistics are hard to come by even in the matters of legal transfers: information on sensitive issues such as defense is sometimes reluctantly publicized in full, and that which reaches statistics can be inaccurate for a number of reasons. For instance, dual-use goods may fall out of defense sales inventories,[45] while different accounting standards for definite defense items preclude accurate estimates, as most registers collect information on a voluntary basis and sometimes fail to provide detailed definitions of arms transfers (e.g., the UN Register of Conventional Arms), leaving it to states' discretion to determine what qualifies as an arms sale.[46]

Small arms exports, due to their relatively low dollar value, may not even be reflected in official statistics,[47] while estimates of the global trade in small arms and light weapons range from $5 billion to $7 billion a year, with some running as high as $10 billion.[48] And while official statistics indicate that the trade in major weapons systems has fallen sharply with the end of the Cold War, many analysts believe that global transfers of light weapons have increased during this period.

Whereas the fabrication of major weapons systems is highly concentrated, with only a dozen or so states capable of producing modern tanks, war planes, and warships, over 300 manufacturers in some 50 countries (including a dozen or more developing countries) now manufacture light weapons and/or ammunition of various types. Estimates of some common models produced by these countries in the past few decades show the enormity of the problem: 5 to 7 million Belgian FAL assault rifles produced in 15 countries; 35 to 50 million Soviet/Russian AK machine guns manufactured by Soviet/Russian factories and licensees, with 6 million more made in China; 7 million German Heckler & Koch G3 assault rifles made in 18 countries; and 8 million US M-16 rifles produced in seven countries.[49]

45. Anthony, 'Trends in Post-Cold War International Arms Transfers', p. 26.

46. Anthony, 'Introduction', p. 13.

47. Ibid., p. 11.

48. Keith Krause, 'Constraining Conventional Arms Proliferation: A Model for Canada,' *Multilateral Approaches to Non-Proliferation*, Andrew Latham, ed. (Toronto: York University 1996), p. 57.

49. Virginia Hart Ezel, 'Small Arms Proliferation Remains Global Dilemma', *National Defense* January 1995, pp. 26–27.

These numbers only include the new production, while analysts agree that most of the trade in small arms concerns used weapons.[50] Thus, millions of surplus arms have been sold or given away at the end of the Cold War, when the world's major military powers and NATO and former WTO states found themselves with excess production capacity and/or weapons stocks following the reduction of their armed forces. Accordingly, countries such the United States, Russia and states of the former Soviet Union, Germany (especially with the disbanding of the East German Army), and the East-Central European former WTO members transferred millions of light weapons to their allies and clients abroad.[51] It is generally acknowledged that a significant portion of these arsenals ended up in zones of armed conflicts (such as Ethiopia and Eritrea, Former Yugoslavia, Kashmir, the Middle East, or Africa).

It is widely believed that after the dissolution of the Soviet Union, many arms producing companies, traders and even military commanders in Russia and some of the former Soviet republics have engaged in large-scale legal and illegal sales of weapons, exploiting the absence or weakness of arms export control regimes.[52] Government officials in other states have been accused of smuggling arms to allied groups in other countries, whether for profit or the advancement of particular political, national, or religious objectives.

To give a few examples, Russian police statistics name theft of weapons from military warehouses among the main sources of weapons appearing in the black market. In most cases the officers and soldiers enter the illicit arms trade themselves or conspire with black-market dealers or criminal groups.[53] Sometimes government officials engage in dubious arms deals, as for example, in the 1994–95 affair when the Tallinn garrison commandant and head of the Estonian General Staff financial department organized the import and sale of $170,000 worth of firearms and ammunition from the Finnish company Ultramatic OY, with the help of a bribed border guard.[54]

50. *Small Arms Survey* (2001).

51. See *Arms Control Today*, August/September 1998, p. 17.

52. Cf. Anthony, 'Illicit Arms Transfers'.

53. Authors' archives.

54. Tallinn *ETA News Agency* in English, 0845 GMT, 21 June 2001; Helsinki *Helsingin Sanomat* in Finnish, 26 September 1995, p. 5 (www.nisat.org), accessed 4 April 2003; *Postimees*, 21 June 2001 (http://www.postimees.ee/index.html?number=770&op=lugu &id=23979).

Although officially no arms are being exported by Estonia, the Russian Federal Counterintelligence Service at one time (1995–96) had identified Estonia as a major regional arms exporter with trade connections leading to Russia's criminal circles, Chechen rebels, former Soviet states, the Balkans, and Somalia in the times of crises there, and even IRA paramilitaries.[55] Estonia, naturally, has denied such accusations, claiming that Russia was trying to present it as a semi-criminal state in order to undermine its national prestige, and accused Russia of supplying arms to the IRA in its turn.[56] A chain of arms traffickers operating through legally established companies in Poland, Latvia, and Estonia that had illegally exported over $4.5 million worth of small arms and ammunition from Poland was disclosed in 1999 as a result of cooperation between Polish and Estonian criminal investigators and intelligence services.[57]

As follows from these examples, the weapons black market is highly criminalized, with strong linkages between arms and human trafficking and the illicit narcotics trade, which all fuel various types of low-intensity conflict.[58] These issues are difficult to address, because in many cases the illegal structures have intertwined with the legal ones, leading to a phenomenon known as "mafiocracy," or system mafia. The connection is reciprocal, with government officials being tempted to exploit the loopholes in legislation or control over the established practices on one side, and criminal organizations establishing legal facades to cover their illegal activities, on the other.[59] Nonetheless, awareness of these problems is rising worldwide, with calls to set up measures being issued by various international organizations and individual states. The next section will offer an overview of efforts designed to curb the unchecked proliferation of weapons.

55. *Literaturnaya Gazeta*, No. 11, 15 March 1995, p. 13 (www.nisat.org). accessed on 4 April 2003.
56. Moscow *NTV*, 1800 GMT, 8 May 1996, (www.nisat.org) accessed on 4 April 2003.
57. *Rzeczpospolita*, 6 January 2000, page A4, (www.nisat.org), accessed on 4 April 2003.
58. cf. Anthony, 'Illicit Arms Transfers'.
59. Jürgen Roth, 'Organiseeritud Kuritegevus Narko-, Relva-, ja Inimkaubanduse Vallas' (Organized Crime in the Sphere of Illegal Drugs, Weapons, and Human Trafficking), paper presented at the 9th Forum Balticum Conference, Tartu, September 1999, (http://www.forumbalticum.ee/konv9/roth_e.htm), accessed on 2 April 2003.

## ADDRESSING THE THREAT OF UNCONTROLLED PROLIFERATION: INTERNATIONAL, EUROPEAN AND NATIONAL EFFORTS

The post-Cold War period has witnessed several multilateral initiatives to control weapons proliferation, with the 1990–91 Gulf War providing a powerful incentive to revise the habitual practices of the arms trade. It was only logical that the permanent members of the UN Security Council concerned themselves with the problem of arms sales to potentially unstable regions, as three of the five—Russia, France, and the UK—were the source of the bulk of Saddam Hussein's arsenal. The resulting P5 Guidelines for Conventional Arms Transfers (1991), although a partial measure (as France was only to happy to see China pull out of negotiations over more binding arrangements following US arms supplies to Taiwan),[60] was an important milestone on the way to a set of international regulations currently in place.

Measures to control weapons transfers can be subdivided into two broad groups, one addressing legal proliferation (Krause's "primary circuit"), and another illicit and illegal transfers (the "secondary circuit").[61] The first group includes national or multilateral export policies (including the codes of conduct), national policies on weapons possession, control and oversight of production and stockpiles, reductions of weapons stockpiles, weapons marking and transparency measures, and regional codes of conduct and registers. The second group of measures comprises tightening and harmonizing export control systems and policies, increasing international transparency, establishing tighter control over private arms dealers, brokers, and transporters; prohibiting international transfers to non-state actors, as well as building the capacity of weak states to monitor activities within their own territory.[62] Apparently, the "points of policy intervention" into the primary and secondary circuits of proliferation complement each other, as the legal and illicit trade are linked in a number of ways, with "a sharp distinction between licit and illicit transfers impossible to draw."[63] Increasing transparency and reducing ambiguities

60. See Kortunov, op. cit., pp. 98–99; Durch, op. cit.
61. See Krause, 'Small Arms and Light Weapons'.
62. Keith Krause, 'Small Arms and Light Weapons', pp. vi–vii.
63. Ibid., p. vi.

surrounding the legal trade will help reveal the routes by which the arms are diverted into the illicit circuit, which in itself is far more difficult to control, due to its covert character and transborder (and often global) reach.

*International Measures*

Policy-makers have begun to highlight the need for strengthening the international efforts to fight the illicit light arms trafficking. Secretary-General Kofi Annan noted that it was time to translate the awareness of the problem of small arms and light weapons into decisive action to reduce the volume of transfers.[64] The Panel of Governmental Experts of the UN produced the Report on Small Arms and the Crime Prevention, and the Criminal Justice Division of the Economic and Social Council came out with the International Study on Firearm Regulations.[65]

To supplement the UN Convention Against Transnational Organized Crime, the United Nations General Assembly on 1 June 2001 adopted without vote a Protocol on the illicit manufacturing of and trafficking in firearms, their parts, components, and ammunition. The protocol was opened for signing from 1 July 2001 to 12 December 2002, although it is not yet in force. The first international instrument to deal with firearms beyond the regional level, the protocol provides for the identification and tracing of each firearm produced by States Parties and sets a framework for intergovernmental cooperation. However, it is limited in scope, focusing only on the involvement of organized crime. (In this respect, the Protocol is essentially the same as the Convention signed in1997 by members of the Organization of American States on the illicit manufacturing and trafficking of firearms.)

The 2001 UN Conference on the Illicit Trade in Small Arms and Light Weapons in All Its Aspects adopted a consensus Programme of Action to Prevent, Combat, and Eradicate the Illicit Trade in Small Arms and Light Weapons in All Its Aspects. The measures

64. *Report of the Panel of Governmental Experts on Small Arms*, Report #A/52/298, from the Secretary General to the UN General Assembly, 27 August 1997. *Measures to Regulate Firearms for the Purpose of Combatting Illicit Trafficking in Firearms*, UN Economic and Social Council, Vienna, 28 July 1998.
65. Ibid.

adopted include strengthening the national regulations governing the production and transfer of small arms; ensuring marking of weapons by manufacturers to enable tracing of seized weapons; improving the system of end-use certification; increasing security of stockpiles; cooperating with the UN system to ensure effective implementation of Security Council arms embargoes, and encouraging cooperation with relevant international and regional organizations and NGOs.[66]

Although smaller in its geographical scope, the 1996 Wassenaar Arrangement includes world's major arms producers, including several countries of East-Central Europe (Bulgaria, Czech Republic, Hungary, Poland, Romania, Russia, Slovakia, and Ukraine).[67] It provided a document setting out non-binding guidelines for transfers of conventional arms and dual-use goods and technologies, also calling upon members to subject small arms and light weapons to national export controls.

At their latest plenary, the 33 countries participating in the arrangement approved a British proposal to identify "best practices" for exporting small arms and light weapons. Although the "decision to transfer or deny transfer of any item"[68] continually resides with the participating states, the guidelines provide the exporters with criteria to be used when assessing the implications of possible sales and situations in which exports should be refused. For instance, when considering a possible export, Wassenaar members are encouraged to weigh the importing country's compliance record with arms control and non-proliferation regimes, as well as its respect for human rights. Other considerations are whether the potential buyer can afford the weaponry and whether it has legitimate need for such arms. Exports should be avoided if Wassenaar members believe there is a risk of weapons ending up in the hands of terrorists or organized crime, if the arms could prolong or aggravate an ongoing conflict, or if they could be diverted to another country. Members further agreed that weapons recipients should inform the original exporter before re-exporting any imported small arms or light weapons

66. *Small Arms Survey: Counting the Human Cost* (2002, at http://www.smallarmssurvey.org/Yearbook/EngPRkitCH5_11.06.02.pdf), accessed on 3 April 2003.
67. Wassenaar Arrangement homepage (www.wassenaar.org/list/wa-list...), accessed 26 September, 2003.
68. Ibid.

and that exported small arms should be individually marked so they can be traced.

*European Measures*

Among European countries, there is an increased pressure for controlling both legal and illegal shipment of weapons, particularly to countries experiencing civil strife and human rights abuses. In June 1997 the EU agreed to a Program for Preventing and Combating Illicit Trafficking in Conventional Arms. In June 1998, the EU formally adopted a Code of Conduct on Arms Exports to areas of conflict and internal repression. The EU Joint Action on Small Arms (December 1998; officially 15 January 1999) envisages both preventive and reactive measures, and creates a framework for providing financial and technical assistance to control small arms transfers, although measures to remove and destroy ammunition do not fall within its scope.[69]

"Region" in terms of arms proliferation routes may differ from the more traditional geographical images of regions,[70] just as it does from the perspective of regional security ties.[71] Thus NATO measures, particularly those introduced through wider fora (such as the Euro-Atlantic Partnership Council), have significant bearing for Europe. The alliance has been engaged with the issue of small arms since the April 1999 Washington Summit. An *ad hoc* working group, set up in July 1999, identified 3 areas requiring enhanced contribution, such as:

1. generic training on stockpile management and security; the collection, disposal, and destruction of weaponry; and small arms control in peace missions;
2. tailored assistance and cooperation: support for individual countries to develop their border control, stockpile management and

69. *Small Arms Survey* (2001), pp. 270–271.
70. 'Potential Regional Action and Policy', in *Controlling the Availability and Unlawful Use of Arms at the International Level: The United Nations and Civil Society* (http://www.nisat.org/default.asp?page=publications/pub_videos.htm, 1998), accessed 10 September 2003.
71. Barry Buzan, Ole Wæver, & Jaap de Wilde, *Security: A New Framework for Analysis* (Boulder, CO: Lynne Rienner, 1998); Durch, op. cit.

security, export control regimes, and customs and police enforcement; and
3. best practices: information exchange, consultation on transparency, and weapons marking regimes.[72]

Checks by the OSCE whether the information submitted by its member states according to the Vienna document (1999) regarding the existing stockpiles and location of military bases is correct is an important transparency measure.[73] The initiatives of the Geneva Center for the Democratic Control of Armed Forces (DCAF, founded in 2000), covering the countries of Europe, as well as the US, South Africa, and Nigeria, likewise aim to reform, and enhance the transparency of, the signatories' security sectors.[74]

*National measures*

National and multilateral levels of activity complement each other in establishing regulatory regimes, as without national control multilateral measures hardly yield any results, and multilateral regulation, on the other hand, prompts harmonization and standardization of unilateral efforts.[75] While global efforts (such as the UN measures) apply to the European countries evenly (depending, of course, on the degree of their commitment as well as their share in "contributing" to the problems in question) and generally have a voluntary character (owing, obviously, to the difficulties of enforcement, both practical and legal), the requirements of regional organizations such as the EU or NATO are obligatory for their members and candidate countries. Harmonization of export policies and improvement of implementation capacities have therefore been prominent on the agendas of many East-Central European states. Estonia, for example, has been developing its laws on import, export and transit of strategic

72. *Small Arms Survey* (2001), pp. 273–274.
73. *Postimees*, 23 October 2002 (http://www.postimees.ee/index.html?number=770&op=lugu&id=76425), accessed on 3 April 2003.
74. See the Geneva Center for the Democratic Control of Armed Forces web site (http://www.dcaf.ch), accessed 6 October 2003.
75. *Small Arms Survey*, (2002), (http://www.smallarmssurvey.org/Yearbook/EngPRkitCH6_11.06.02.pdf).

goods, including dual use items, during 1994–2001,[76] with an explicit orientation to the EU legislation.

While introducing compatible tight legislation based on improved understanding of the effects of uncontrolled proliferation of weapons (such as escalation of conflicts, curbing of development initiatives, links with other types of organized crime, etc.) is an important measure, to be effective it should be coupled with the development of implementation capacities (which for many countries represents a greater problem than introducing legislation itself).[77] Increasing the efficiency of border control constitutes an important policy direction, as it reduces the opportunities for the traffickers to engage in their illegal activities by enabling oversight of migration and trade.

For EU states and candidate countries, national efforts are built into a wider framework of EU measures, such as the Schengen Information System (SIS) and the proposed setting up of European Border Police and a European Corps of Border Guards,[78] which span the areas of national and European jurisdiction in administrative as well as financial terms. Infrastructural and technical assistance to the prospective EU members' border control facilities has been of great value, as it also enhances the security of the neighboring states.

For the EU's neighbors, especially Russia with its remote and porous borders,[79] strengthening border control to prevent illicit weapons movement also remains a high priority. It is to be hoped that Russia's new (and long awaited) military doctrine will, by ascertaining the priority directions in the development of its armed forces, contribute to more consistent allocation of resources into both the development of weapons and related technologies and control over their "leakage."[80] The Balkan states—another region with reportedly

76. 'Strateegiliste Kaupade Nimekiri' [List of Strategic Goods] (http://trip.rk.ee/cgi-bin/thw?$%7BBASE%7D=akt&$%7BOOHTML%7D=rtd&ID='VVm_RT_I_2001,_44,_243', accessed 3 April 2003.

77. See 'Potential Regional Action and Policy', ibid.

78. Kristina Ojuland, 'Eesti piirivalve Euroopa Liidu julgeolekupoliitika komponendina' (The Estonian Border Guard as a Component of European Security) , 29 October 2002 (http://www.vm.ee/est/euro/kat_46/2965.html), accessed 4 April 2003.

79. Anthony, 'Illicit Arms Transfers'.

80. e.g., Kortunov, op. cit.

problematic borders—are receiving some assistance through the DCAF project on border security systems, whose 12th Meeting on "Logistical Support, Including Budgetary Issues in Border Security" took place in Tallinn in October 2003.[81]

## CONCLUDING REMARKS

Based on the above, it is possible to state that regarding weapons proliferation, policies are tailored to counter the perceived threats to post-Cold War security and stability, in Europe as well as worldwide. The notable trend in these policies is the desire to prevent weapons diversion to non-state actors, either directly, through illicit sales, or indirectly, through violations of end-user undertakings. The range of measures thus covers exports of both conventional and light weapons and small arms, as well as related equipment, materiel, technologies, and various dual-use goods. Additional emphasis is placed on clearer understanding of the characteristics and sources of contemporary conflict, with the policy instruments being gradually brought into correspondence with the nature of problems they are intended to address.

Still, notwithstanding the calls for decisive action, the change in approaches and attitudes to weapons proliferation appears slow, due to both institutional inertia and understandable reluctance on the part of states to compromise what they perceive as their vital interests. Despite the abundance of initiatives to control arms transfers, they do not make up a coherent body of policies, with responsibility and resources scattered among various international and regional organizations and individual states who sometimes experience coordination problems. It is important, however, not to underestimate the policy tools developed at various levels of (inter)national regulation, for although piecemeal handling of security problems has its drawbacks, it is perhaps more realistic with regard to the concrete tasks various agencies take upon themselves to perform, than a broad but inefficient institutional framework would be: after all, the jurisdiction

81. The Geneva Center for the Democratic Control of Armed Forces web site (http://www.dcaf.ch/news/upcomingevents.htm), accessed 6 October 2003.

over weapons-related security issues may be the last sphere in which the states are prepared to relinquish control.

Coupling disarmament and weapons proliferation control initiatives with other, softer policies—such as development and community (re-)building programs—as part of the general peacebuilding effort, on the other hand, deserves close consideration, although attention should be paid to local needs and expectations in order to ensure the efficiency and sustainability of the undertaking.[82]

With regard to the effectiveness of the measures described, it seems likely that the coordination of efforts at controlling arms proliferation in Europe as a whole will mostly impact on the situation outside the region (the Balkans being perhaps the closest problematic spot in mind here, but also Central Asia and the Caucasus with their ties to the Middle East, and Africa, among the closest of Europe's neighbors), as it is there that the illegal flow of arms is mostly directed. And the situation there, in turn, will have repercussions for the countries of Europe, upon which instability in the neighboring regions, in one way or another, will inevitably rebound. Therefore, while thinking in terms of Europe as an integrated region (formal institutional links apart) is a considerable step forward compared to the situation a decade ago, the political ramifications of its wider ties have largely yet to find adequate reflection in European countries' routine policy concerns.

82. Tamara Duffey, 'Cultural Issues in Contemporary Peacekeeping', pp. 142–168 in Tom Woodhouse and Oliver Ramsbotham (eds.), *Peacekeeping and Conflict Resolution* (London and Portland, OR: Frank Cass, 2000).

# DEFENDING THE FORTRESS? ASSESSING THE EUROPEAN UNION'S RESPONSE TO TRAFFICKING

DAVID BROWN

## INTRODUCTION

The European Union's (EU) institutional landscape is littered with policy initiatives, strategies, and draft proposals regarding trafficking. These occasionally contradictory initiatives have developed, in part, because no consensus exists within the EU as to the best way to approach this multi-faceted problem. While some countries have cast their net globally, considering factors such as poverty and political instability, others have considered factors closer to home, namely the failure to effectively implement existing measures, such as the much-maligned Dublin Convention.[1] There is also a geographical facet, with member states focusing on different sources of trafficking depending on their proximity to a known trafficking route.

Consequently, the EU has embraced measures across the spectrum from preventive actions to punitive measures. One proposal in the former category involves creating "safe havens" within the states of origin in order to prevent potential immigrants from journeying to the EU.[2] Carrier sanctions and the harmonization of member states' criminal law, as contained in the Framework Decision on Combating Trafficking in Human Beings (which envisaged penalties of up to 8 years for trafficking for sexual purposes and forced labor)[3] are representatives of the other.

Two specific areas of activity have therefore been selected for in-depth consideration. They are the development of effective border management strategies, of particular importance given the current enlargement process, and the contribution made by the European Police Office (Europol). In the former, given the wealth of potential cases to examine, there is a need once again to narrow the focus. This article will therefore concentrate primarily on the impact Poland will have on the EU's external border—"no matter what criteria one uses, Poland is the biggest and most important applicant country."[4] Europol will be assessed both within the narrow confines of the fight against trafficking and also in the more general contribution the agency has made to raising the EU's profile in the already crowded field of internal security.

There are a number of reasons why these particular cases have been selected as appropriate vehicles for an initial assessment. Firstly, both play an important role in fighting illegal trafficking: "the ideal country will be one that can be entered easily and travelled

1. Wille, P. *Future Policies on Prevention of Trafficking of Human Beings in Europe* (http://www.belgium.iom.int/STOPConference/Confdocs/Confpapers 2002; 12 June 2003).

2. Watson, R. 'Britain thwarted on safe havens for refugees', *The Times*, 20 June 2003.

3. Justice and Home Affairs Council, *Council Framework Decision 2002/629/JHA of 19 July 2002 on combating trafficking in human beings - OJ L 203* (Luxembourg: Office for the Official Publications of the European Union 2002).

4. Friis, L. & Jarosz, A., 'When the going gets tough: The EU's Enlargement Negotiations with Poland' (http://www.dupi.dk:80/webtxt/wp9905.html 1999).

across quickly. The quality of its border controls...will therefore be of paramount importance in determining whether traffickers will regard a given state as a suitable transit route."[5]

In addition, Europol has begun to stake a claim to a greater role in border management, taking on a coordinating role in the 2001 High Impact Operation.[6] Their overall importance has also been recognized in relation to the prioritization that has taken place regarding the completion of the Schengen acquis by the applicant states. While a two-stage process has been accepted, with internal frontier controls between existing Schengen states and the applicants remaining beyond accession, both police cooperation and border management are considered essential pre-accession elements.[7]

This symmetry is mirrored in the chronology. Both Europol and the current enlargement process have their genesis in 1991, a year that saw the then German Chancellor Helmut Kohl advocate a European Police Office and Poland and Hungary, the first two applicants from Central and Eastern Europe (CEE), sign their initial Europe Agreements. The two approaches are also representatives of potentially competitive processes of European integration, namely deepening and widening, prompting some speculative comments on the effectiveness of attempting to inter-twine two occasionally divergent policy processes.

## AROUND THE HOUSES

Following an extended delay in agreeing a draft External Frontiers Convention within the auspices of the then European Community (EC), a solution was discovered in the Schengen acquis—the 1985 Schengen Agreement and the subsequent 1990 Schengen Implementation Convention (SIC). As part of the 1999 Treaty of Amsterdam, this acquis was absorbed into the EU acquis, and its provisions regarding the external frontier became the standard that applicant states would have to meet.

---

5. Europol Management Board, *Crime Assessment: Trafficking of Human Beings into the European Union* (The Hague: Europol 2002).
6. Sjolinder, N. *Trafficking in Human Beings: The European Response* (http://www.belgium.iom.int/STOPConference/Confdocs/Confpapers/ 2002; 12 June 2003) p. 19.
7. Vandamme, L. 'Schengen and integration of Schengen into the European Union with a view to Enlargement', *Collegium* No.22 (2001) p. 116.

For example, Article 6 (2b) SIC states that: 'all persons must be subject to at least one check making it possible to establish their identities', while a later clause calls for 'an equivalent level of control... (to) be exercised at external frontiers'.

This wording does not close off the possibility of a more pessimistic interpretation, namely an agreement to the lowest common denominator of control. While this may seem like pedantry, it is actually of some importance when considering the level of effectiveness that the EU is attempting to enforce. Words are important, especially within the EU, where each statement has been the subject of patient negotiation between 15 members and so has been carefully selected to represent the agreed compromise of occasionally starkly differing positions—"the political culture of Europe is inevitably based on compromise."[8] In addition, a Common Manual was established, containing further standards regarding the efficiency of surveillance, the level of staffing, and the adequacy of cooperation with neighboring states.[9] While these documents have been augmented further, with new additions including the Schengen Catalogue,[10] a legally non-binding set of best practices in this specific area, the initial principles have escaped relatively unscathed.

Before considering the specific case of Poland, it is worth taking a brief tour d'horizon of some of the other acceding states. Although in no way a comprehensive survey, this will give some indication of the scale of the problems that still remain to be resolved if the Justice and Home Affairs (JHA) acquis regarding border control is to be met in full. It also places Poland's efforts within a wider context, demonstrating that Poland cannot be considered an exceptional case. Most of the examples are drawn from the Commission assessment undertaken in October 2002; as this will form the basis on which

8. Tony Blair, 'Speech by the UK Prime Minister to the US Congress on 17th July 2003', *Hansard* 2003.

9. For further details, see the Schengen Executive Committee, *The Schengen Standing Committee: A Decision of the Executive Committee on 16th September 1998* (http://www.statewatch.org/semdoc/file/NEW/STANDCT.HTM 9 May 2000).

10. See European Council, *European Union Schengen Catalogue: External Border Control—Removal and Readmission: Recommendations and Best Practice* (Luxembourg: Office for the Official Publications of the European Union 2002).

final judgements regarding accession are made, it is the most appropriate source material to utilize.

- In Estonia, the Commission considered that on the ground activities were "functioning satisfactorily." This is a somewhat optimistic assessment, given that the same report accepts that "staffing levels in the Border Guards are a particular concern in the medium term," with the consequence that "the targets of the Schengen action plan risk not being met."[11] This is also not a new criticism. In 1999, the Commission assessed that it would take at least nine years to meet Schengen standards,[12] taking Estonia well beyond not only the accession deadline of 2004, but also the proposed transitional period whereby internal frontier controls would remain while Estonia was within the EU.[13] Given that this has not been refuted, it can only be assumed that the original negative assessment stands.
- With an estimated 10% of all migrants entering the EU via the Balkans,[14] Slovenia will be of considerable importance in tackling the threat of trafficking. There are signs that it has recognized this, with changes made to its Schengen Action Plan regarding recruitment, a problematic area for most applicants. However, this is balanced by the fact that Slovenia had not, at the time of writing, implemented any specific legislation with regard to trafficking.[15] It is also worth noting a general point regarding the nature of the

11. Commission of the European Communities, *Regular Report from the European Commission on Estonia's Progress Towards Accession on 09.10.02*, (Luxembourg: Office for the Official Publications of the European Union 2002) p. 103.

12. Commission of the European Communities, *Regular Report from the Commission on Progress Towards Accession by Estonia on 13.10.99*, (Luxembourg: Office for Official Publications of the European Communities 1999).

13. The German State Secretary, Mr Diwell, believed the transition period would last for 2 years—see House of Lords, 'Select Committee on the European Union Twenty-Ninth Report: Proposals for a European Border Guard HL 133', *Hansard* 2003.

14. Bruggeman, W. *Illegal Immigration and trafficking in human beings seen as a security problem for Europe* (http://www.belgium.iom.int/STOPConference/Confdocs/Confpapers/2002; 12 June 2003.

15. Holmes, P. & Berta, K. *Comparative Matrix on Legislation and Best Practice in Preventing and Combating Trafficking in Human Beings in EU Member States and Candidate Countries* (http://www.belgium.iom.int/STOPConference/Confdocs/Confpapers/2002; 12 June 2003).

Commission's assessment in this area. With the final deadline of a process declared by the EU to be "irrevocable"[16] approaching, it was not satisfactory that assessments are based on incomplete information—"it is too early to assess the effects of changes to Slovenia's capacity to ensure the required level of border control."[17]

- There is better news in relation to the Czech Republic, which demonstrated substantive success in intercepting illegal immigration at its borders. However, its "special relationship" with neighboring Slovakia may undermine the Czech Republic's successes. As former constituent parts of Czechoslovakia, border management between the two states has been minimal. This border, now an internal EU border, with Slovakia becoming the primary external border guard. Slovakia, while making the necessary institutional and legislative changes required to satisfy the *formal* acquis, still has "serious problems with regard to illegal immigration."[18] As potential traffickers are likely to seek out the weakest link in the chain, Slovakia's failure is of far greater concern than its neighbor's success story.

## THE POLISH PROBLEM

An assessment that resonates across the board—with the exception of Hungary, which received an unqualified positive report card in 2002—relates to the issue of staffing. Poland is no exception, with the most recent report concluding that "staffing problems in the Border Guard remain."[19] This long-term structural problem has yet

16. European Council, *Presidency Conclusions from the Gothenburg European Council on the 15/16.06.01*, (Luxembourg: Office for Official Publications of the European Union 2001) p. 2.

17. Commission of the European Communities, *Regular Report from the European Commission on Slovenia's Progress Towards Accession on 09.10.02*, (Luxembourg: Office for the Official Publications of the European Union 2002) p. 102.

18. Commission of the European Communities, *Regular Report from the European Commission on Slovakia's Progress Towards Accession on 09.10.02*, (Luxembourg: Office for the Official Publications of the European Union 2002) p. 107.

19. Commission of the European Communities, *Regular Report from the European Commission on Poland's Progress Towards Accession on 09.10.02*, (Luxembourg: Office for the Official Publications of the European Union 2002), p. 113.

to be fully resolved. In 1999, the Commission declared itself unable to conclude when Poland would meet the relevant acquis, as there was "no overall plan . . . which can quantify . . . the number of years needed for achieving even the minimum standards currently expected."[20] The following year, a substantial shortfall in the Polish Border Guard was noted, with only 18,000 of the 25,000 posts filled (approximately 35% vacancies).[21] Whilst this gap may have been reduced slightly by 2002, when a 30% gap was recorded,[22] resolving this issue is proving a very slow process indeed. At the present rate, it will take some considerable time before the Polish Border Guard is operating at full capacity, in part because of the low salary scales associated with such work.[23] The Polish government is not unaware of this problem. Bold commitments have been made, to increase the number of border guards by over 5000 by 2006,[24] which would fall in line with the informal timetable advocated by some for the final completion of the transitional Schengen phase. However, judging on the past record, a certain amount of scepticism is justified on hearing such pronouncements.

Additional factors complicate this already poor situation. First, the issue of corruption needs to be addressed. While this is in no way a uniquely Polish condition, or even one limited to the applicant states, it cannot be avoided when considering staffing levels. It is insufficient simply to consider this matter at the quantitative level. The qualitative element must also be considered in assessing

20. Commission of the European Communities, *Regular Report from the Commission on Progress Towards Accession by Poland on 13.10.99*, (Luxembourg: Office for Official Publications of the European Union 1999).

21. European Parliament, *Report on Poland's Application for Membership of the European Union and the State of Negotiations on 20.09.00*, Luxembourg: Office for the Official Publications of the European Union 2000) p. 12.

22. Commission of the European Communities, *Regular Report from the European Commission on Poland's Progress Towards Accession on 09.10.02*, (Luxembourg: Office for the Official Publications of the European Union 2002) p. 119.

23. In Estonia, for example, Border Guards are rated 72nd amongst all state employees with regard to pay. See Evisalu, A. *The Estonian Border Guard—Working Paper No. 4* (Geneva: Geneva Centre for the Democratic Control of the Armed Forces 2002) for more details.

24. Lungescu, O. 'Poland to Buttress Expanded EU borders' (http://news.bbc.co.uk/1/hi/world/europe/2162090.stm; 24 June 2003).

whether widening the external border to embrace the CEE states is a step towards the stated aim of the EU to effectively combat all forms of trafficking. In 1997, the International Crime Victim Survey indicated that, along with the Czech Republic, Poland had the highest level of corruption of any state recorded.[25] This judgment was reinforced by the Commission, which concluded in 2000 that not only was there a significant problem, but also that "regrettably, there is a general lack of a long-term and integrated anti-corruption strategy in the public administration."[26]

Subsequent reports have, however, noted that the subject was being taken much more seriously within Polish governmental circles. The 2002 report noted a significant rise in the number of corruption related arrests, a welcome comment (although also indicative of the scale of the problem). Mutual confidence in the competence of other member states' internal security agencies will remain a key element underpinning the external frontier regime. Therefore, even a perception of lingering corruption is likely to have a damaging impact on the willingness of existing member states to trust the Polish frontier guards to discharge their responsibilities competently.

This could, in part, help to explain the decision to maintain internal frontier controls between existing Schengen states and the applicant states for an undisclosed "transitional" period beyond formal accession. As yet, the Schengen states do not possess the necessary confidence to fully integrate Poland within Schengen. Instead, a decision will be taken, by unanimity, at a later date. This is seen as providing an incentive to accession states to speedily complete the legal and administrative acquis to the satisfaction of existing members. However, it is equally possible to see such a decision in entirely the opposite light, as a disincentive to reform, especially when taken in conjunction with some other statements regarding the enlargement process. For example, the EU had already declared, before the final assessment had taken place, that enlargement was an irreversible process, given the length of time, commitment and credibility that

25. Siemaszko, A. *The International Crime Victim Survey in Poland: 1996* (Warsaw: Ministry of Justice 1996). Russia was not included in the survey.

26. European Parliament, *Report on Poland's Application for Membership of the European Union and the State of Negotiations on 20.09.00*, Luxembourg: Office for the Official Publications of the European Union 2000).

had been invested by all sides. Enlargement is always spoken about in grandiose, heroic terms—"we will see few more significant events in our lifetime."[27] Given that the conclusion of the process is known, for perfectly understandable political reasons, it is difficult to see how this can act as an incentive for further reform.

The new member states will possess a much larger degree of institutional leverage post-accession, particularly in the Third Pillar, where the unanimity rule continues to apply. (This Pillar, a series of new competencies and new institutions established to tackle the soft security threat at a regional level and create an "area of freedom, security, and justice" by 2004, was established as part of the Maastricht arrangements.) Once inside, by a combination of tactical voting and issue linkage, Poland could make life very difficult for the EU across a whole spectrum of issues. Arguably, having been treated as a second class member in relation to Schengen, there is little incentive for the Poles—and other future members—to meekly accept further perceived humiliations. Within the area of border management, there is evidence of Poland striking a distinct note, separate from the EU's existing priorities. For example, there is the proposed "Eastern Dimension," regarding states that will neighbor the EU's new external frontier. Here, Poland has called for a far less severe approach to be taken, even hinting that "the EU might consider some flexibility in the visa regime" that is currently being enforced. This could easily become a bargaining chip in the institutional negotiations that characterise the EU's high, and occasionally, low politics. The zenith of the existing member states' influence over this process occurred before, not after, accession. The comments of the German State Secretary should also be remembered: he hinted that the transition period would last little more than two years after accession,[28] not, in itself, enough time to fully rectify the problems highlighted in the Commission's own assessment.

The argument also supposes that states such as Poland were primarily interested in meeting the terms of the acquis as currently laid down. There is evidence to suggest that Poland is not

27. Tony Blair cited in Straw, J. *EU Enlargement: Enlightened Self-Interest* (London: Foreign and Commonwealth Office, 2002).

28. House of Lords, 'Select Committee on the European Union Twenty-Ninth Report: Proposals for a European Border Guard HL 133', *Hansard* 2003.

convinced of the need to strengthen its eastern border, especially at the expense of the western frontier with Germany (which is now an internal EU frontier). At present, the Border Guard is almost evenly split between the two, despite the fact that 'the pressure on the eastern border remains substantial."[29] While new recruits are immediately allocated an eastern frontier role, the substantial recruitment gap suggests that this is little compensation, especially in the short term.

In addition, as Colonel Kasinski, the Deputy Commander in Chief of the Polish Border Guard noted, because of the cost factor involved, there was no plan to relocate existing staff from the western and southern borders.[30] Poland may thus not necessarily view a continued exclusion from Schengen as a great hardship. When considered alongside Poland's attitude towards another element of border management, namely the establishment of friendly relations with neighbouring states, such a position is even more convincing. The policy also runs counter to the EU's longer-term aspirations in this area.

## IN THE NEIGHBORHOOD

Poland has long held the opinion that a toughening of the external frontier regime, the so-called "ring of steel," was counter-productive.[31] It feared that a much tighter visa regime, coupled with a strengthening of border controls, could have a deleterious effect on both diplomatic and economic relations within the region, making tackling cross-border

29. Commission of the European Communities, *Regular Report from the European Commission on Poland's Progress Towards Accession on 09.10.02*, (Luxembourg: Office for the Official Publications of the European Union 2002), p. 114/115.

30. House of Lords, 'Select Committee on the European Union Twenty-Ninth Report: Proposals for a European Border Guard HL 133', *Hansard* 2003.

31. It is not alone in feeling this. In 2003 the Commission has produced a document calling for the establishment of a 'zone of prosperity and a friendly neighborhood'. See Commission of the European Communities, *Communication from the Commission to the Council and the European Parliament: Wider Europe—Neighborhood: A new Framework for Relations with our Eastern and Southern Neighbours COM (2003) 104* (Luxembourg: Office for the Official Publications of the European Union 2003) p. 4.

threats such as trafficking more, rather than less, difficult. In the course of the accession process, Poland has tried not to apply such regulations in full, committing itself instead to a policy whereby the Polish border would "remain open for economic and cultural co-operation, and for the development of relations between peoples."[32] President Kwasniewski has repeatedly stated that Poland is not prepared to implement a visa regime with Ukraine,[33] although such a policy will have to be implemented in due course. Yet, given Poland's stated position, there can be no guarantee that, Poland will implement pre-existing EU policy.

There is also a case to be made for non-adherence, or, at least, a softer line in relation to neighboring states, given that "a border cannot be controlled from one side only."[34] This is a position accepted in the Schengen Catalogue and is in line with the initial Schengen acquis, which stated that "agreements with neighboring countries… in the field of border management are an efficient tool in increasing border security."[35] Yet, by insisting on tighter visa arrangements and further checks, themselves part of the overall Schengen acquis, there is a real risk that such friendly relations could be jeopardised. Poland's concerns regarding the impact of such measures on the viability of cross-border trade between Poland and Ukraine have already been demonstrated. In 1997, when Poland attempted to seal its border, in order to meet one part of the Schengen standard, cross-border trade fell by approximately 30%.[36] This prompted the Ukrainian

32. See European Council, *European Union Schengen Catalogue: External Border Control—Removal and Readmission: Recommendations and Best Practice* (Luxembourg: Office for the Official Publications of the European Union 2002) for more details.

33. President Kwasniewski cited in Grabbe, H. *The Sharp Edges of Europe: Security Implications of Extending European Union Border Policies Eastwards* (Paris: Institute for Security Studies of the Western European Union 2000). p. 15.

34. Mr Jarvio cited in Bruggeman, W. *Illegal Immigration and Trafficking in Human Beings Seen as a Security Problem for Europe* (http://www.belgium.iom.int/STOPConference/Confdocs/Confpapers/2002; 12 June 2003.

35. European Council, *European Union Schengen Catalogue: External Border Control—Removal and Readmission: Recommendations and Best Practice* (Luxembourg: Office for the Official Publications of the European Union 2002) p. 13.

36. Grabbe, H. *The Sharp Edges of Europe: Security Implications of Extending European Union Border Policies Eastwards* (Paris: Institute for Security Studies of the Western European Union 2000) p. 15.

President, Leonid Kuchma, to complain that, "The European Union is replacing the Iron Curtain with a paper curtain across Europe."[37] In addition, Poland's initial attempts to bring its visa regime in line with Schengen standards was labelled, both by Ukraine and Belarus, as an "unfriendly act," with Belarus even going as far as temporarily withdrawing its ambassador from Warsaw.[38] Given that the long-term success of any policy will depend, in part, on the goodwill of such states, such outbursts—possibly just for diplomatic consumption—are not encouraging. Until the fundamental contradiction at the heart of Schengen is resolved in favor of one policy option or the other, confusion will reign, with an effective border policy a likely victim.

In addition, the financial impact on the region cannot be ignored. Given that one of the underlying causes of trafficking is poverty within the state of origin and, more importantly, the relative disparity between potential starting point and destination, a policy that may, inadvertently, make such a situation worse seems counter-productive at best and politically perverse at worst. This has been recognized within the Commission—"The economic situation in these countries has had a direct effect on the flow of trafficking."[39]— However, the implications of this policy decision does not seem to have filtered through to the higher echelons of the European Council.

The 2002 Seville Conclusions on Asylum and Immigration included the following statement:

> 'The Council may unanimously find that a third [non-EU] country has shown an unjustified lack of co-operation in joint management of migration flows. In that event the Council may . . . adopt measures or positions under the Common Foreign and Security Policy and other European Union policies, while honouring the Union's contractual commitments and not jeopardising development co-operation objectives.'[40]

---

37. Ibid, p. 17.

38. See European Council, *European Union Schengen Catalogue: External Border Control—Removal and Readmission: Recommendations and Best Practice* (Luxembourg: Office for the Official Publications of the European Union 2002).

39. See Europol Management Board, *Crime Assessment: Trafficking of Human Beings into the European Union* (The Hague: Europol 2002) p. 1.

40. European Council, *Presidency Conclusions from the Seville European Council on 21–22.06.02* (Luxembourg: Office for Official Publications of the European Union 2002).

Such strong statements may make good media headlines, but they are not a substitute for clear and coherent policy. Suggesting some form of "punishment policy" for states that do not adhere to expressed EU standards contradicts the efforts to establish a "friendly neighborhood"; it cannot be considered an effective solution to the problem.

## SHARING THE BURDEN?

That is not to say that this area is short of potential solutions to some of the problems outlined above. If anything, the opposite is the case: there is an abundance of competing answers, each attempting to alleviate the perceived strain on the applicant states through slightly different permutations of "burden sharing."[41] This element of current discussion of border management acts as a microcosm of the wider field of trafficking—while there may be a consensus as to the existence of the problem, there is no agreement as to the most effective way to counter it. Consensus may exist at the level of principle, but this has not permeated down to the level of practical response. Instead, differing diagnoses vie for institutional time within an already crowded agenda.

Belgium, for example, has concentrated on legal harmonization, stating that "to tackle a phenomenon it is a conditio sine qua non to have a legal framework almost comparable in every European state."[42] This would prevent a "weakest link" appearing in the chain for the potential trafficker to exploit.

Other solutions look outside the legislative field, concentrating instead on practical manifestations of burden sharing, such as

---

41. See, for example, Commission of the European Communities, *Communication from the Commission to the Council and the European Parliament: Towards Integrated Management of the External Borders of the Member States of the European Union—COM (2002) 233* (Luxembourg: Office for the Official Publications of the European Union 2002); European Council, *European Union Schengen Catalogue: External Border Control—Removal and Readmission: Recommendations and Best Practice; Plan for the Management of the External Borders of the Member States of the European Union on 14.06.02* (Luxembourg: Office for the Official Publications of the European Union 2002).

42. Wille P. *Future Policies on Prevention of Trafficking of Human Beings in Europe* (http://www.belgium.iom.int/STOPConference/Confdocs/Confpapers/2002; 12 June 2003) p. 6.

manpower, equipment and financial support. For example, the Commission, supported by Germany, advocates a European Border Guard, which it hopes will be operational within four or five years of accession. However, the UK actively opposes such a proposal, preferring a much looser, informal arrangement, perhaps based on bilateral exchanges of liaison officers.

The Italian Feasibility Study offered an additional solution, a "network centric model" of different networks within each member state that would form a "virtuous circle that allows an increase of reciprocal trust and the possibility to exploit... knowledge on a larger scale."[43] Not as radical as the Commission proposal, accepted in the study as the "final goal" of efforts in this area (although on a significantly different timetable), it was an institutional step beyond what the UK was advocating. While accepting that national budgets will remain the mainstay of financing in this area, the study also called for a common fund, organized on the basis of the member states' respective Gross National Products (GNP), rather than, at present, on a quirk of geography. It is worth considering some of these proposals in greater depth, to see whether any of them provide a viable means of alleviating the burden that currently rests on the shoulders of those geographically on the EU's periphery.

The Belgian proposal centres on the idea of legal harmonization. With the Framework Decision mentioned earlier, a significant step has been taken towards just such an objective, with a set of common penalties agreed for specific elements of the overall trafficking phenomenon. However, only the eventual destination for the member states is set; how they arrive at such an end within their legal frameworks is a matter of national discretion. Given the disparate positions that exist, both in terms of where the burden of the problem lies and the differing severity with which it is currently handled in countries' penal codes, arriving at a common destination may prove exceptionally difficult.

A comparative matrix of human trafficking legislation was devised in 2002, covering both existing member states and the CEE

---

43. European Council, *Feasibility Study for the Setting up of a European Border Police, Plan for the Management of the External Borders of the Member States of the European Union on 14.06.02* (Luxembourg: Office for the Official Publications of the European Union 2002) p. 36.

applicants.[44] It makes very interesting reading. For example, of existing members, only Denmark had legislation that criminalized all elements of trafficking. At the other end of the scale, Finland, France, Germany, Italy, and the UK had no specific anti-trafficking legislation, although, in the last three states, legislative processes were underway. Different member states criminalized different aspects, based, in part, on the elements that most affect their own national territory, with some focusing on the trafficking of children (Ireland and Luxembourg), while others, such as France, concentrated on prostitution. In addition, the penalties attached varied substantially, ranging, in the case of trafficking minors for prostitution, from a maximum of 3 years in Greece to 20 years in Italy.

The situation was made even more complex when the applicant states were added to the picture. No details regarding sentencing were provided for Latvia, Lithuania, or Slovenia, making it difficult to assess the overall picture. In addition, their inclusion widened the scope of potential offenses (Estonia refers only to unlawful prostitution and Bulgaria to kidnapping, whereas Poland refers to "offences against sexual liberty and decency"). Once again, EU widening has a potentially deleterious impact on the deepening of legislation to counter trafficking. States tend to be protective of their own criminal legislation, believing their way to be the most effective. The task of even approximating harmonization of such a disparate picture may not be possible in the time-frame laid down by the EU, which aims to report on member states' efforts in this area by 1 August 2005.

The Commission was also hopelessly optimistic in arguing that some form of European Border Guard system, which would run alongside national Border Guards and be supplemented by a common fund and, potentially, common equipment, should be in place within the next five years.[45] In its defense, the Commission can point to some successful bi- and multilateral initiatives, such as that which took place on the Polish-German border in December 2002, involving

44. Commission of the European Communities, *Regular Report from the European Commission on Slovenia's Progress Towards Accession on 09.10.02*, (Luxembourg: Office for the Official Publications of the European Union 2002) p. 102.

45. Commissioner Antonio Vitorino is quoted in Monar, J. *The Project of a European Border Guard: Potential, Models and Challenges* (Geneva: Geneva Centre for the Democratic Control of the Armed Forces 2003) p. 13.

German, Italian, and British volunteers.[46] However, there is a difference between a flexible, state to state, voluntary exchange, that is limited in both duration and scope, and an additional permanent European institution, as advocated by the Commission.

Questions have been asked as to how such a system would operate in practice. Mention has been made, for example, of a corpus of equipment to be made available for use at the common external frontier, although not of the ownership of such material. The UK has also raised issues regarding its transport. The issue of financing remains a potent one. Whilst additional funding has been supplied through projects such as PHARE, the record with regard to JHA specific projects does not encourage great optimism—"Much of the PHARE funds used…go into internal market reforms of the administration and judicial systems, rather than be focused on specific JHA diversity projects."[47] With limited resources and innumerable competing priorities, the majority of funding is likely to be targeted at those areas considered most important for ensuring a smooth accession. An unintentionally revealing comment by the Commission advocated that states such as Ukraine should "be offered the prospect of a stake in the EU's Internal Market," in order to establish a "zone of prosperity" beyond the EU's borders, noting: "If a country has reached this level, it has come as close to the Union as it can without being a member."[48] This confirms the primacy of economic factors in the accession process and suggests that the funding needed to alleviate the burden at the external frontier is unlikely to be automatically forthcoming.

In relation to manpower, there does not seem to be a great desire on the part of the existing members to move beyond the

---

46. For details, see Holmes, P. & Berta, K. *Comparative Matrix on Legislation and Best Practice in Preventing and Combating Trafficking in Human Beings in EU Member States and Candidate Countries* (http://www.belgium.iom.int/STOPConference/Confdocs/Confpapers/2002; 12 June 2003).

47. Monar, J. *EU Justice and Home Affairs in the Eastward Enlargement: The Challenges of Diversity and EU Instruments and Strategies—ZEI Discussion Paper C91* (Bonn: ZEI 2001) p. 26.

48. See Grabbe, H. *The Sharp Edges of Europe: Security Implications of Extending European Union Border Policies Eastwards* (Paris: Institute for Security Studies of the Western European Union 2000) p. 10.

voluntary level, as in the case of the exchange of airport specialists[49] or the Rapid Reaction Unit.[50] The UK is completely opposed to anything that smacks of institutionalizing burden sharing, advocating a process of building on existing capacity, rather than "having to think about constructing some almost monstrous legislative bureaucratic structure."[51] It was not alone in opposing a European Border Guard; significantly, and evidently overlooked in the internal discussions that have taken place, certain applicant states were also opposed to such a move. They object to the idea of officers from other states operating on their territory, believing that "each one should try to protect their own borders."[52] As enlargement takes root, the balance is likely to swing further in their direction. Certainly, it will be very difficult to implement such a proposal in the face of opposition from the very states that would be expected to play host.

## EUROPOL—AN INSTITUTION IGNORED?

There is little point in the EU committing itself to a further bout of institutional advancement if the very states that are supposed to benefit most from it are, at best, agnostic about its merits. Even if states such as Poland and the UK were prepared to permit the creation of such an agency, their disinclination to utilize its services is likely to ensure the latest addition to the crowded EU institutional landscape is stillborn. The record of Europol stands as testimony to indulging in a strategy that places institution building over implementation. It is worth considering in a little more depth not only the lessons that could be learned from Europol's experience over the past decade, but also the contribution that this most prominent example of deepening integration has made in countering trafficking in all its forms.

49. See European Council, *Plan for the Management of the External Borders of the Member States of the European Union on 14.06.02*, (Luxembourg: Office for the Official Publications of the European Union 2002) p. 16.

50. European Council, *Feasibility Study for the Setting up of a European Border Police*, (Luxembourg: Office for the Official Publications of the European Union 2002) p. 72.

51. Lord Filkin cited in Bruggeman, W. *Illegal Immigration and Trafficking in Human Beings Seen as a Security Problem for Europe* (http://www.belgium.iom.int/STOPConference/Confdocs/Confpapers/2002; 12 June 2003).

52. Colonel Kasinski cited ibid.

Antonio Vitorino, JHA Commissioner, has lamented that, "National governments, when asked what they are doing to combat that type of crime, frequently answer that Europol has now been given the competence to deal with it and that therefore the problem is solved."[53] It is not enough simply to allocate another competency to Europol, or create a further agency to tackle the problem—this is to confuse activity with accomplishment. It can also prove counter-productive. Not only has the allocation of continued competencies to Europol's mandate given the member states a false sense of security in relation to how it is handling problems such as human trafficking, but it also creates a problem of prioritization within the organization. Europol, at present, is being asked to cover a substantial array of soft security problems, without the budget or the manpower to effectively manage its ever-expanding mandate. This situation is only likely to worsen as enlargement brings new states with new problems to the table.

It is not only member states that make demands, as the agency also has to respond to the changing international security environment. This has led to terrorism rising up Europol's priority list, at the expense of all other areas, in the wake of September 11th 2001—"Most other work was temporarily frozen as the majority of resources were put into efforts…focusing on extreme Islamic terrorism."[54] While this is to be expected, such changes do not take place in isolation, and there are always consequences, in terms of available manpower and resources, for other competing items on the agenda. Although there are signs that some states are finally realizing the problematic situation that they have created, this is a case of shutting the barn door after the horse has bolted. No one is suggesting lightening Europol's load; rather, certain subjects will simply have to fall by the wayside while the agency deals with other things.

Despite the continued expansion of the agency's mandate, there has been no commensurate improvement in Europol's performance

53. Vitorino, A. *Speech by the JHA Commissioner to the Europol Conference organised by the Senate and House of Representatives of the Dutch States General — 'Democratic Control of Europol' on 08.06.01* (Luxembourg: Office for Official Publications of the European Communities 2001).

54. Europol Management Board, *Annual Report for 2002: Report on the Activities of Europol in 2002* (The Hague: Europol 2003).

in its main contribution to the field of internal security, namely information exchange. While greater efforts are being taken to promote an operational role for Europol, the bulk of the agency's activity is still to be found in the collection, processing, analysis, and exchange of information. Europol is still totally dependent on the member states providing initial raw information, as it has no collection facilities of its own. This information is then analyzed and stored in central databases, available to all member states on request. Both the provision and requesting of information provide key indicators of Europol's continued utility in the eyes of the people who created it, namely the member states. Yet, in both cases, having established this route of information exchange, beyond the less formal channels that were already available, the member states have failed to follow through on their initial enthusiasm. It is worth taking each in turn.

First, in the provision of information, the record is sadly lacking. One example concerning human trafficking will suffice to demonstrate this. Europol had been asked to provide an assessment of the scope and scale of human trafficking, including a quantitative analysis of the problem, rates of flow and geographical grouping. However, Europol had to admit defeat—"on the basis of the data received from the member states, this has not been entirely achievable." This is an understatement. Ten of the 15 member states failed to provide any information at all, with both the UK and Ireland claiming that such phenomena were limited or no problem within their states. It should also be remembered that states such as France and Finland do not consider trafficking a criminal activity, and thus were unable to provide Europol with information. Of the remaining five submissions, Italy's contribution is worth noting. Accepting that "accurate statistics are not available," Italy "guesstimated" the scale of the problem, based solely on the number of foreign prostitutes on its streets, arriving at an approximate figure of 6000–7000. Moreover, its analysis was based on the questionable assumption that all these foreign prostitutes were trafficked into Italy. Germany, in contrast, gave not only a specific figure—926 cases—but also demonstrated the percentage increase over the previous year.

If Europol is to demonstrate that it can provide "added value" in the fight against trafficking, it must have access to comprehensive and accurate information. Instead, it is given a fraction of the data and the tools it requires. This situation is mirrored in states' role as

TABLE I
Europol's Record: Information Requests[55]

| Year | No. of Initial Requests |
|---|---|
| 1994 | 585 |
| 1995 | 1474 |
| 1996 | 2053 |
| 1997 | 2608 |
| 1998 | 2298 |
| 1999 | 2180 |
| 2000 | 1922 |
| 2001 | 2268 |
| 2002 | 2413 |

consumers of Europol's information provision. As Table I—which charts the number of requests for information from the member states since Europol's inception, based on Europol's own figures—demonstrates, it has been a bumpy ride for Europol as it tries to establish itself in the already crowded field of internal security.

The upturn in requests over the past two years has been explained thus: "The extension of the Europol mandate on the one hand and the introduction of liaison officers of non EU countries... have contributed to an overall increase."[56] Europol has begun to receive information from non-EU sources, such as the applicant states and other newly formed EU agencies like the EU Police Chiefs Task Force. The impact of September 11, 2001, should not be underestimated, as Europol took a far more prominent role in counter-terrorist activity than it had done in the previous two years when such matters had been within its institutional ambit. Thus an increase was to be expected. More worrying is the fact that there has not

55. See European Council, *Europol 2000 Annual Report* (Luxembourg: Office for Official Publications of the European Union 2001); European Parliament, *Report by the Committee on Civil Liberties and Internal Affairs on the Annual Report of the Europol Drugs Unit for 1996 on 04.09.98 — PE 227.073*, (Luxembourg: Office for Official Publications of the European Communities 1998), Europol Drugs Unit, *Report on the Activities of the Europol Drugs Unit in...: A Summary* (The Hague: Europol 1997–1998) and Europol Management Board, *Annual Report...: Report on the activities of Europol in...* (The Hague: Europol 1999–2003).

56. Europol Management Board, *Annual Report for 2002: Report on the Activities of Europol in 2002* (The Hague: Europol 2003).

been a continuing growth in the number of requests year on year. It has taken the agency four years to recover the ground that it lost after 1997. This suggests that the current upward trajectory cannot be counted on to continue indefinitely.

## CONCLUSION: CONTRADICTIONS VERSUS CLEAR CHOICES

From even the briefest scan of some of the measures that the EU has begun to put in place to counter internal security threats such as human trafficking, it is clear that there are serious problems. Most stem from the failure of the EU to make difficult, but fundamental, choices regarding the over-arching policy to be adopted. Rather than offer a clear strategic view, the EU—partly because of the inevitable culture of compromise that pervades an organization composed of 15 occasionally disparate views—has fudged issues, offering nudges and winks in different directions instead of clear and consistent leadership. The result has been a counter-trafficking strategy based on a series of contradictions:

- Embracing a hard-line policy with regard to tighter border controls and visa restrictions, while at the same time calling for the establishment of a "zone of prosperity" among good neighbors. This contradiction lies at the heart of the Schengen acquis that the applicant states have been told to implement in full. It also makes the countering of human trafficking more difficult, given the effects on the local economy.
- Promoting "added value" by creating new institutions, without following through the implementation process to ensure that agencies such as Europol have the basic tools to allow them to do their job effectively.
- Promoting the dual strategies of deepening and widening simultaneously, regardless of the effect that one has on the other. Widening to include the CEE states is likely to have an impact on EU policy, particularly in areas such as border management where the problem is likely to increase. As Europol has noted, "Their impending membership of the EU must be seen as a threat with regard to the

> trafficking of human beings."[57] It will also make progress in developing the Third Pillar much more difficult, given the reliance on unanimity. "Fortress Europe," in strengthening the eastern frontier at the expense of what will become internal borders, is also counter-productive.

While such contradictions remain, the EU will be hamstrung in its efforts to counter threats such as that posed by human trafficking.

57. Europol Management Board, *Crime Assessment: Trafficking of Human Beings into the European Union* (The Hague: Europol 2002).

# THE UNITED STATES, EUROPE, AND HOMELAND SECURITY: SEEING SOFT SECURITY CONCERNS THROUGH A COUNTERTERRORIST LENS

JACK CLARKE

Homeland Security in the United States is first, foremost, and always about defending the national realm of the US against terrorism. But Homeland Security also means confronting soft security threats; particularly insofar as they are enablers of terrorism. Securing the homeland is the most important function of the US government.[1]

1. The declaration of the struggle against terrorism as the highest security priority of the US Government is reflected in many official documents appearing since 11 Setember 2001. See, *inter alia*, Office of Homeland Security, *National Strategy for Homeland Security* (Washington, DC 2002), p. 1.

This simple statement is key to understanding the role that homeland security plays in the security strategy of the United States and the impact that the developing approach to homeland security, as well as the institutions being created to support that strategy, are likely to have on the ability of the United States to address the full range of soft security threats. Many soft security concerns will be viewed in the US through this counterterrorist lens, with ineluctable distortions and misperceptions. Inevitably, this focus on countering terrorism means that less attention, and thus fewer resources, particularly with regard to intelligence and law enforcement, will be available to counter the full range of soft security threats. At the same time, this heightened attention to terrorism will result in a paradoxical byproduct of more results in countering the soft security threats.

To effectively address the threat posed by modern terrorism, a homeland security strategy must address these other security threats, as terror groups often leverage them to achieve their goals. This article examines the extent to which the homeland security approach affects the ability of the US to deal with other security threats, notably the range of soft security threats. It will examine the US approach to homeland, or internal, security, with particular attention to the organization and forces developed to provide this security, contrasting the European and US approaches to these challenges. The article also examines the concept of Homeland Defense, as distinct from Homeland Security, and evaluates its impact on the soft security agenda. Lastly, it examines the impact of the US homeland security effort on the traditional European soft security agenda.

## THE US APPROACH TO HOMELAND SECURITY

In the aftermath of the September 11, 2001, attacks in the US, it was obvious that the provisional security regime for defending against internal terrorist threats was not equal to the new challenges. The diffuse nature of the US federal intelligence and law enforcement apparatus, coupled with the hierarchical nature of government, with its national, state, and local levels, served to ensure that defense measures would be porous, and that responses to attacks would be less than optimally coordinated.

There had, of course, been any number of studies and panels warning of potential asymmetric attacks on critical infrastructure; and indeed, there were many intelligence indicators of several kinds of attacks; but there was no one agency responsible for pulling the indicators together and acting on them.[2] These functions had traditionally been dispersed among dozens of federal agencies and thousands of first-responder groups across America. Homeland security, while important to security and law enforcement officials, was simply not on the political agenda.

Homeland security, as set forth in the US National Strategy for Homeland Security, has four objectives: to prevent terrorist attacks within the US; to reduce the vulnerability of the US to terrorism; to minimize damage from those terrorist attacks that do occur; and to recover from such attacks. The emphasis on terrorism is thus clear, and other considerations are subordinate to this focus.[3]

It is important to make a clear distinction between Homeland *Security* and Homeland *Defense*, as these terms are not interchangeable in the US usage. Homeland Security is "the preparation for, prevention of, deterrence of, preemption of, defense against, and response to threats and aggression directed toward US infrastructure, as well as crisis management, consequence management and other domestic civilian support."[4] Homeland Defense, on the other hand, is the protection of US territory, sovereignty, domestic population, and critical infrastructure against external threats and aggression. Whilst it may simplify things to think of Homeland Defense as the military component of Homeland Security, this is not quite correct: Homeland Security is focused on internal threats, while Homeland Defense looks outward at external threats.[5]

Homeland security, which appears at times to be an awkward construct, is also not quite the same as interior or domestic security, as might be the case in the European context. It is critical to note at

2. See, *inter alia*, the *Roadmap for National Security; Imperative for Change*, the Phase III Report of the US Commission on National Security in the 21st Century (Hart/Rudman Report), available at www.nssg.gov/phase III.pdf.

3. Office of Homeland Security, op. cit., p. 3.

4. Ibid. See also US Joint Chiefs of Staff, *Joint Doctrine for Homeland Security*, (JCS Publication 2-26 [draft], Washington DC 2002).

5. U. S. Joint Chiefs of Staff, Pub 2-26 (draft).

the outset that the US organizational solution for homeland security should not be equated with a typical European ministry of the interior. There are significant differences, most notably in the focus on terrorism and the lack of a law enforcement capability, that would make this comparison somewhat misleading, as will be explained.

## THE CHALLENGE OF HOMELAND SECURITY IN THE US

The enormous challenge of ensuring the domestic security of a country the size of the United States is perhaps best expressed by some figures: the United States has some 12,000 kilometers of land borders; and over 150,000 kilometers of coastline and navigable waterways, as well as over 5.5 million square kilometers of exclusive economic zone adjacent to the coastline. It has nearly 250 international seaports and over 400 international airports. Every year, over 500 million people enter or exit the US, as well as 16 million freight containers, part of over $2 trillion in international trade.[6]

These figures, though they focus principally on border and transport security, give a useful idea of the dimensions of the challenges as they relate to soft security concerns as well as terrorism. The tremendous vulnerability portrayed in these figures represents a signal opportunity for those who wish to exploit America's openness for criminal gain.

Prior to September 11, 2001, the security of this realm was divided both horizontally with shared jurisdiction spread over several cabinet ministries and dozens of federal agencies; and vertically through the 97,000 government units found in the three principal layers of government. Those government units employ over 650,000 law enforcement officers, whose coordinated efforts are essential to securing the homeland. Moreover, intelligence activities could be found at many levels and in many organizations. Due to legal prohibitions, domestic intelligence collection and dissemination is very difficult, and intelligence sharing between and among agencies has been woeful, as demonstrated in the investigations following the September 11 attacks. In addition, owing to the fears of a too-powerful national government, the US lacked a powerful ministry of the interior, with

6. Office of Homeland Security, op. cit., p. 8.

control over a national police force. Law enforcement remains very much a state responsibility, and no national police force exists (the FBI being principally an investigative agency).

Of equal interest, with the exception of limited air defense and an incipient missile defense system, there was no organization within the US military specifically charged with the defense of the home territory. North America was not part of the area of responsibility of any of the US geographic commands that circle the globe.

## ORGANIZING FOR HOMELAND SECURITY

*A Ministry of Internal Security?*

To oversee the security of this realm, and to coordinate and consolidate this disparate effort as well as to better coordinate the government's response to a range of other threats, President Bush signed legislation on November 25, 2002, creating the Department of Homeland Security (DHS). The intent was to streamline and centralize all national-level (federal) actions focused on domestic security into one cohesive unit. In addition, the Department is intended to provide a single point of contact for state (provincial) and local (municipal) governments, as well as the private sector.[7]

The DHS has five critical mission areas:

- Intelligence and Warning
- Border and Transportation Security
- Protection of Critical Infrastructure and Key Assets
- Defending Against Catastrophic Threats
- Emergency Preparedness and Response.[8]

While all of these mission areas are concerned with soft security threats and challenges to some extent, it is evident that they focus principally on terrorism and its consequences. To the extent that soft security concerns are a part of this mission focus, it is likely to be as a secondary, if still important, concern.

7. U S Department of Homeland Security (DHS) web site (www.dhs.gov).
8. Office of Homeland Security, op. cit, p. 11.

It has been noted that the creation of the DHS is the largest reorganization of government in the US in the more than 50 years, indeed since the creation of the Department of Defense in 1947. Twenty-two federal agencies, with nearly 170,000 employees, have been amalgamated into the DHS. These include many agencies on the front lines of the struggle against soft security threats, such as the Immigration and Naturalization Service, the Customs Service, and the Transportation Security Administration.[9]

The DHS has established four policy-oriented directorates and one for management. The four policy directorates, which closely track the critical mission areas, include:

- Border and Transportation Security
- Emergency Preparedness and Response
- Information Analysis and Infrastructure Protection
- Science and Technology.

### *Securing Modern Border and Transport Systems*

The Border and Transportation Security Directorate is the one most directly concerned with soft security threats. In addition to its principal mission of securing the borders and ports-of-entry of the United States, it also has principal responsibility for protecting the transport infrastructure, as well as administering US immigration and customs laws. In addition, it has responsibility for enforcing the nation's agricultural laws at the international borders of the United States.[10]

To better understand the Directorate's role with respect to soft security threats such as illegal immigration, smuggling, and human trafficking, it is useful to review how the Directorate approaches the issue of border security. The basic principles of modern secure borders are a recognition that open borders are a key to commerce, but that people, ideas, and goods and services must be able to flow in a secure environment, while ensuring that these borders remain closed to terrorists and criminals.[11] There is a clear recognition that the

9. DHS web site.
10. DHS web site.
11. Remarks by DHS Under Secretary Asa Hutchinson at the Chamber of Commerce for Latin America conference, 7 May 2003.

Directorate cannot inspect every person, vehicle, and package entering the US. Therefore, the strategy of the Directorate is to push borders forward, in the sense of beginning the secure borders process in the countries of origin, as well as increasing the depth of borders, by enforcing immigration and customs laws within the territory of the US. To achieve this strategy, the Directorate has three entities charged with executing its mission:

- *Bureau of Customs and Border Protection*, which functions as the nation's gatekeeper, presenting a single face at borders and ports of entry, and provides security against illegal entry.
- *Bureau of Immigration and Customs Enforcement*, which acts as the nation's interior line of defence, and is charged with intelligence, interdiction, and investigation functions related to enforcing US customs and immigration laws.
- *Transportation Security Administration*, which has responsibility for securing all US transport systems, including aircraft and ships originating in foreign countries.

The Directorate of Information Analysis and Infrastructure Protection is responsible for all information and intelligence functions within the DHS, and thus has direct authority for overseeing the nation's critical infrastructure. Because so much of the infrastructure of the world's developed economies is electronic, and thus subject to relatively easy manipulation by perpetrators of soft security crimes and schemes, this directorate plays a key role in confronting these threats.

Likewise, the Directorate of Science and Technology is certain to play a major role in helping to develop technology solutions that can assist in managing soft security threats, particularly as they relate to law enforcement and forensic issues. In much the same way that the US Department of Defense's technology efforts have spurred significant investment in defense-related technology, spending on homeland security technology will have important impacts on the efforts to manage soft security challenges.

In addition to these directorates, three organizations with significant soft security responsibilities have been absorbed into the DHS as separate entities. These are the United States Coast Guard, the United States Secret Service, and the Bureau of Citizen and Immigration Services.

The Coast Guard is intimately involved with pressing the campaign against terrorism as well as defending against soft security threats. It maintains a significant overseas presence and carries out its port security and exclusive economic zone enforcement missions not only in the US, but overseas as well, by beginning the intelligence and interdiction missions in foreign ports.[12]

Likewise, the Secret Service, in addition to protecting the integrity of the US currency, also has responsibility for crimes associated with major financial institutions, including credit fraud, money laundering, and telecommunications fraud. Thus, the Secret Service plays a critical role in addressing economic threats. Recently, the Secret Service cooperated with Romanian law enforcement authorities to break up a major Internet fraud operation.[13]

The Bureau of Citizenship and Immigration Services, also an independent service within the DHS, has key responsibilities for regulating the flow of immigration to the United States. It is responsible for determining immigrant status, authorizing visas, and processing asylum seekers and refugees. It is thus is a key player in soft security issues such as illegal immigration, human trafficking, and abuse of asylum and refugee status.[14]

While terror remains the first priority of the DHS, the department inherited many other responsibilities not necessarily related to this primary mission. For example, the Coast Guard remains responsible for maritime safety, waterways management, aid to navigation, and protection of natural resources. Other agencies absorbed into the DHS also retain their original responsibilities, and must seek to balance

---

12. The Coast Guard remains a military service as well as a law enforcement agency, subject to mobilization in wartime. In addition, it performs numerous missions associated with maritime safety and environmental safety. See US Coast Guard web site (www.uscg.mil).

13. For information on the Romanian cyber crime connection, see Kole, William J. "Romania's Internet Vampires Prey on the World," *Los Angles Times*, 26 October 2003. For additional information of the US Secret Service, see US Secret Service web site (www.secretservice.gov).

14. The DHS will now deploy agents to Muslim countries to screen visas applications in cooperation with the US State Department. See Shenon, Phillip, "Homeland Security Department Planning 7 Offices Overseas to Screen Visas," *The New York Times*, 7 October 2003. See also US Bureau of Citizenship and Immigration Services web site (www.immigration.gov).

their anti-terror efforts with their mission of providing a broad range of public services.

*Other US Soft Security Agenda Players*

Despite this major consolidation of security-oriented agencies within the DHS, other departments of the US government retain significant responsibility not only with respect to the campaign against terror, but also with regard to other soft security threats, particularly in a foreign context. The creation of the DHS did not, it must be emphasized, create a "one stop shop" for coordination of efforts against soft security threats. These include the Department of State, the Department of Justice, the Department of the Treasury, the Department of Commerce, and the Department of Energy, with its oversight of nuclear weapons.

Of these, the Department of Justice remains a major, indeed principal, player in the national effort against soft security threats. Several of its subordinate organizations are in the front line. The Federal Bureau of Investigation (FBI), the Drug Enforcement Administration (DEA), and the Bureau of Alcohol, Tobacco and Firearms (ATF) are the most prominent of these, along with the US National Central Bureau of INTERPOL, responsible for coordinating US activities with INTERPOL.[15]

The FBI, though not a national police force, has major federal law enforcement responsibilities. The FBI is, exceptionally, active outside the United States, and maintains numerous overseas offices. Since the attacks of September 11, 2001, the FBI has undergone a major re-orientation to focus on combating terrorism within the US. The FBI also has principal responsibility for investigating terror acts directed against US citizens outside the US, and thus is leading US efforts in countries such as Iraq and Indonesia.[16] The DEA is the principal US agency combating the trafficking in illegal drugs and illicit substances, as well as the financing associated with these activities.[17] Likewise, the

15. US Department of Justice Web site (www.usdoj.gov).

16. See Bravin, Jess and Adams, Chris, "Justice Department to Shift Resources to Fight Terror," *The Wall Street Journal*, 9 November 2003, p.4., See also US Federal Bureau of Investigation web site (www.fbi.gov).

17. US Drug Enforcement Administration web site (www.usdoj.gov/dea).

ATF is in the forefront of US efforts to combat illegal trade in small arms and explosives, all key soft security concerns.[18]

In addition, it is obvious that the Department of Defense remains a major player in this arena, given its intelligence and offensive counterterrorism capabilities. Moreover, the department, because of its worldwide deployments and long-range intervention capabilities, is intimately involved with managing soft security threats. Moreover, it is the principal agency responsible for the provision of Homeland Defense, and thus has a major role in confronting soft security threats.[19]

The Department of the Treasury, through its Executive Office for Terrorist Financing and Financial Crime, as well as its Office of Foreign Assets Control plays a major role in investigating and enforcing US and international actions with respect to the financial aspects of soft security threats. These agencies are specifically charged with enforcing economic sanctions and freezing the US-based assets of terror and criminal groups.[20]

Lastly, the Department of Commerce, through its Bureau of Industry and Security, is responsible for nonproliferation and export control cooperation activities, as well as administering industry compliance with the Chemical Weapons Convention and assisting with chemical weapons verification regimes.[21]

As a consequence, while the DHS houses many of the agencies concerned with addressing soft security problems and challenges, it shares that responsibility with other agencies; coordination of effort, particularly in the area of intelligence sharing, remains a problem. Many of these agencies retain their own intelligence services; a new effort to integrate these efforts, the Terrorist Threat Integration Center (TTIC), began operations on 1 May 2003. This center serves as a clearinghouse for intelligence regarding potential terrorist attacks, but clearly also receives and analyzes significant amounts of information related to soft security threats. It is designed to integrate the terrorism-related intelligence capabilities of the FBI, CIA, DHS, Department of Defense, and Department of State. The TTIC is

18. Bureau of Alcohol Tobacco and Firearms web site (www.atf.gov).
19. US Department of Defense web site (www.defenselink.mil).
20. US Department of Transportation web site (www.dot.gov).
21. US Department of Commerce web site (www.commerce.gov).

scheduled to move to new premises, co-located with the FBI's Counterterrorism Division and the CIA's Counterterrorist Center, thus providing a major intelligence center focused on terrorism and, by extension, other soft security threats.[22]

*The Coordination Conundrum*

The melding of so many disparate, and in some instances dysfunctional agencies into a single entity has, understandably, not been without problems. The current effort to combine three separate agencies (Customs, Immigration, and Border Patrol) into a single, seamless border security apparatus is a case in point. Each of the agencies coming to the DHS has its own corporate culture and business approach; developing a single culture is proving to be a Sisyphean task. Also, the decision to leave several agencies, such as the Coast Guard and Secret Service, as independent agencies under the DHS umbrella has proven troublesome in terms of coordination of effort. And as we have seen, there remains a plethora of federal agencies with important domestic security responsibilities outside the DHS, making an interagency approach to security essential. No one agency can do it all.

Nor can one government do it all. The federal nature of government in the US means that close coordination between the levels of government is essential, given that local and state governments provide most of the law enforcers, as well as the first responders in cases of terror attacks. Likewise, these governments enforce many laws that directly affect the ability of the US to defend itself against soft security concerns.

Thus, there remain major hurdles in terms of developing the right kinds of interagency and interministerial linkages and coordination channels for homeland and soft security issues. In this regard the European experience can be instructive. As Jonathan Stevenson has noted, France's highly effective intelligence coordination system, in which the *Secretariat Générale de la Défense Nationale* coordinates the effort of both the judicial and executive branches, offers some

22. The White House, *Fact Sheet on US Terrorist Threat Intelligence Center* (Washington, DC 2003).

important lessons for the US as it begins the process of interagency coordination in domestic security matters.[23]

*The European Example*

As noted, the Department of Homeland Security, with its almost exclusive focus on the threats posed by terrorism, has no exact duplicate in Europe. Indeed, the term "homeland" has been the source of significant confusion in Europe. Most of the functions of the DHS are found across a range of ministries in European countries. In most instances, the functions of the DHS would normally be found in either the ministry of the interior (MOI) or ministry of justice (MOJ). The task of securing the homeland is most often described by European equivalents such as "inner" or "domestic" or "internal" security. Most importantly, the DHS is heavily focused on dealing with the threat posed by catastrophic terrorism; and its enforcement capabilities remain very modest compared to a European MOI, which typically exercises suzerainty over most, if not all, of a state's law enforcement elements.

These points of differentiation have implications for cooperation between the United States and its European partners on soft security issues. As a large number of working relationships have been established over the years between European ministries and the US departments of Justice, State, and Transportation on key homeland and other soft security issues, these must now be reestablished with DHS interlocutors. In the short term, many of these individuals may be the same as before, but their focus has clearly shifted. In the longer term, these relationships must adjust to the new paradigm of countering terrorism first.

Moreover, DHS, which now has responsibility for enforcing immigration and customs policy, which are often the source of much friction between the US and Europe, must now endeavor to develop sound relations with foreign partners on law enforcement and combating terrorism. These efforts will require extraordinary levels of diplomacy and cooperation, and it is not yet clear how the DHS will

23. Stevenson, Jonathan, 'How Europe and America Defend Themselves', *Foreign Affairs*, March/April 2003, p. 90.

interface with those organs of the US government charged with other aspects of foreign and security policy.

It will take time for these relationships to become settled and for information exchanges to be routine. Almost inevitably, many will view the DHS's emphasis on combating terrorism as an impediment or distraction to efforts to counter the broader range of soft security threats. This is likely to be particularly evident in the effort to share intelligence, in that there may be some reluctance to share intelligence on soft security threats, for fear it may compromise counterterrorist operations. And, as noted, the US DHS is not the sole, or in some instances, even the preferred provider of cooperation on soft security matters. It will still be necessary to reach out to other agencies of the US government to fully coordinate such efforts.

## EUROPEAN VERSUS AMERICAN COUNTERTERRORISM EXPERIENCE

To understand how this major reorganization and reorientation of the US government will impact on European perceptions, policies, and efforts regarding soft security threats, it is useful to review the fundamental differences between the European and American approaches to combating terrorism. European countries have long been confronted by a range of terrorist threats that have required responses involving the military, law enforcement, and intelligence. The European experience with managing these threats can offer some insights into the dimensions of the challenge and some possible solutions. Yet, while there is much to be learned in examining Europe's approaches to these issues, it is important to recognise that the European experience with terrorism, especially as it manifested itself in the 1970s and 1980s, differed in fundamental ways from the threat of catastrophic terrorism posed by organizations such as Al-Qaeda.

In particular, the objectives of these home-bred terror groups differed fundamentally from those of contemporary transnational groups, in that they did not necessarily seek the destruction of a state or its government, but rather sought changes in policy or increased levels of autonomy or perhaps independence. As a consequence, they were not necessarily interested in causing major loss of life, as that might prove counterproductive to their cause. Consequently, the European experience is different, and different lessons can be drawn from it. The fact is that, given their long experience, Europeans feel strongly that they understand terrorism and its causes better than countries that have never been confronted with these threats. There is a widely held belief that the terrorism threat can be managed and that negotiations, not force, are the preferred solution to dealing with this threat.[24]

These attitudes have been shaped not only by the European experience with the politically motivated terrorism of the 1970s and 1980s, but also by the large minority populations, especially Muslim, which live in many European countries. Some European politicians fear that any actions taken against extremist elements of those societies could result in a backlash and further radicalization. Given the size of these populations, including more than 15 million Muslims in Western Europe alone, this represents a source of serious concern.

As a consequence, many Europeans see the struggle against terrorism in a decidedly different way from most Americans. They tend not to see themselves "at war" against an amorphous terrorist threat; nor do they necessarily see themselves as targets of Al-Qaeda violence and, indeed, many take exception to the US characterization of the effort to combat terrorism as a military operation. Many European opinion leaders evince a visceral dislike of the Global War on Terrorism (GWOT) construction.[25] Some of those opinion leaders, and substantial minorities of public opinion in some countries, hold the view that the US brought the 9/11 attacks on itself, notably by those policies related to support of Israel. There is a sense that participation with the US in the GWOT will make them targets, despite evidence already of numerous terror attacks, both planned and executed, against European citizens and interests by Al-Qaeda and its allies.[26] However, the European experience with terrorism differs in fundamental ways from that of the US. No European country has experienced the kind of catastrophic

24. Shapiro, Jeremy and Bénédicte, Suzan, 'The French Experience of Counter-Terrorism', *Survival*, Vol. 45, No. 1, Spring 2003, pp. 67–68.

25. Stevenson, p.77.

26. Stevenson, p. 78. This point was reinforced in interviews with senior British government officials, 9 September 03.

terrorism that has been directed against the US. Were this the case, it is likely that they would now perceive the threat in a different light. This may account for the differences in approaches to meeting the terrorism challenge.

### *Defending the Homeland*

Among the many key points of convergence and dissimilitude between Europe and the US on the issues involved in securing the realm and defending the homeland is the question of what the proper role of the armed forces should be in managing these challenges. In many countries, the armed forces carry out a broad range of missions and tasks in support of law enforcement. Often, these involve reinforcing activities undertaken to reduce vulnerability to soft security threats. A classic example is the use of armed forces to reinforce border security—an activity found in many European countries. Another is using military assets to track and interdict contraband smuggling. There are many reasons why armed forces are called upon to assist in these tasks. The armed forces usually represent a readily available force with at least some training that is transferable to law enforcement requirements. And they are cheap—in many instances, conscripts are used for this purpose, providing a nearly cost-free alternative to expensive border security forces. Austria's employment of army units to patrol its external EU border is a prime example of this.

Of particular interest is the approach that many European countries have taken with regard to the key requirements of what is now described as Homeland Defense (HLD). HLD is essentially a subset of the much broader Homeland Security (HLS) mission. The Homeland Defense mission, as set forth in recent doctrinal publications of the United States armed forces, focuses on the role that military and other armed security forces play in assuring key elements of homeland security and, by extension, defense against soft security threats.[27] HLD missions include a broad range of military activities, many of them directly related to supporting soft security. In addition to its most fundamental mission, that of the defence of territorial sovereignty, the HLD rubric contains:

27. US JCS Publication 3-26 (draft), 2002, p. I–13.

- Air and missile defense
- Protection of space-based assets
- Protection of cyber systems
- Critical infrastructure protection (CIP)
- Continuity of government (COG) operations.

As noted, Europeans have been executing HLS missions for decades, and their experience is instructive. In particular, many European countries have extensive experience in HLD missions, even though the HLD mission set does not find itself expressed in quite the same way as in the United States. This is particularly true as regards the core HLD mission of sovereignty defense. Europe's postwar security experience until the fall of communism was focused on sovereignty defense. It is ironic that, just as this mission has become a key US interest, it is of declining importance in Europe. Most European countries do not sense that they are threatened by external powers, and have reduced the importance of territorial defence in their strategic calculations. Germany, for example, recently promulgated a security doctrine that makes it clear that the defense of German territory is no longer the highest priority for the German armed forces.[28]

For many reasons, such a shift is long overdue, and resources spent on maintaining legacy defense forces can clearly be spent more profitably elsewhere. However, the core mission of defending territorial sovereignty remains, even if it is no longer considered to be a priority mission. As a consequence of this downgrading, it is generally no longer performed by active forces. Instead, in many instances it has been relegated to a reserve force mission. However, at the same time, there has been a general reduction in reserve forces in most European countries, even those that rely on a militia system, such as Austria and Switzerland.[29]

This subtle differentiation is also apparent with regard to the defense of space and cyber systems. While clearly the provenance of the Department of Defense in the US, space and cyber defence is

---

28. German Ministry of Defence, *Defence Policy Guidelines*, May 2003, p. 4.
29. The International Institute of Strategic Studies, *The Military Balance 2003*, (London: OUP 2003).

not yet even much of an issue in most European military security discussions. Some of this may be due to the relative paucity of European military space systems, but it cannot account for the approach to cyber systems. In Europe, this remains very much in the bailiwick of law enforcement agencies, and thus a soft security issue, as opposed to a ministry of defense function.[30]

As regards air and missile defense, most European countries retain an air defense capability, and some even continue to buy aircraft platforms suited to this mission, such as the Eurofighter, but, as with territorial defense, it is being de-emphasised. At the same time, there has been a renaissance in interest in missile defense. Given the portability of some hand held anti-aircraft missiles, this may rightfully be considered a small arms trafficking issue, and thus a soft security concern. In the past few months, there has been a great deal of discussion on possible cooperative ventures in the area of ballistic missile defense, as Europeans leaders recognize their vulnerability to missile attack and, equally important, recognize the determination of the US to proceed with deployment of a missile defense system in the near future.[31]

The mission area in which the European experience is most instructive is that of Critical Infrastructure Protection (CIP). As in the US, there are a number of critical, but vulnerable systems upon which modern states rely in order to function. These systems have become increasingly vulnerable even as they have gained in efficiency due to automation and electronic data management. They now represent highly vulnerable nodes that can offer tempting targets for terrorists. Equally importantly, these systems are often entry or enabling ports for much criminal activity on the soft security agenda, such as credit and identity fraud and financing of criminal enterprises.

The terror movements of the 1970s and 1980s required European governments to devote considerable resources to providing protection of a broad range of potential targets that we now refer to as critical infrastructure. European law enforcement and military forces have long experience in providing security for key government installations and individuals. However, in the US concept, the range of potential

30. US JCS Publication 3-26 (draft), p. III–4.

31. Taverna, Michael A., 'Fresh Look at BMD; Hostility to US Iraq Policy Doesn't Mean Europe Isn't Worried About Weapons of Mass Destruction', *Aviation Week*, 31 March 2003 pp. 54–55.

targets is considerably larger. The US concept distinguishes between national critical infrastructure and defense critical infrastructure. National critical infrastructure includes:[32]

- Agricultural and food systems
- Financial and banking systems
- Transportation systems
- Water supplies
- Vital human services
- Power systems.

Defense critical infrastructure includes critical information assets and power projection capabilities and assets. Critical information assets include command and control networks, defense computer networks and intelligence, and surveillance and reconnaissance (ISR) assets; while power projection capabilities include mobilisation facilities such as seaports and airports and military transport assets, as well as certain strategic military installations. Most European countries recognise the importance and vulnerability of these assets. European governments, faced with a domestic terrorist threat, have provided security for many of these assets, but few have approached the problem in a comprehensive manner. Responsibility for the protection of critical infrastructure is usually divided between the ministry of defense and the ministry of the interior, with many instances of overlapping jurisdiction. This can create serious difficulties in terms of coordination.

### *Forces for Homeland Security Missions*

Unlike the US, with its federal structure and decentralized law enforcement responsibilities, European countries have considerably more options at their disposal for carrying out key HLS tasks. In addition to military forces discussed above, there are many kinds of police forces in various European countries that have significant HLS responsibilities, and which have no direct counterpart in the US system. In particular, most European countries have one or more national police or paramilitary police forces at their disposal,

32. US JCS Publication 3-26 (draft), p. IV–9.

as well as a range of specialized police forces specifically charged with soft security missions. These may include internal security troops, transport police, finance police, and special event security forces.

With the exception of a small number of federal police forces with very limited missions, such as the Defense Protective Service, which guards the Pentagon and other Department of Defense buildings, there is no uniformed federal police force. While there are a number of federal law enforcement agencies charged with homeland security missions, such as the Border Patrol and Transportation Security Administration officers, their writ is extremely limited.

As regards armed forces, European countries have long employed their active and reserve forces in executing key HLS missions. Unlike the US, most European countries maintain large numbers of military formations on their home territory. Relative to the US, European countries have a high density of armed forces relative to population that are available for these missions. And yet it is interesting that very few of these missions are assigned to reserve force structures. It is striking to note the extent to which many reserve forces have disappeared from many European force structures. Several European countries have quietly disbanded large portions of their reserves, citing the lack of external threat as a justification. As a consequence, there is a clear lack of a surge potential in the event of a catastrophic terror attack. For example, Germany's *Heimatchutzbrigaden*, or home defense brigades, were disbanded after the end of the Cold War. They, like many other reserve and militia organizations, would be prime candidates for HLS missions, particularly in the areas of HLD and military support during major disturbances.

On the other hand, many European countries have specialised police forces, which are capable of performing a broad range of homeland security functions. In particular, the paramilitary police forces found in several countries have long experience in carrying out tasks associated with combating terrorism, such as infrastructure protection and special event security, as well as having principal responsibility for domestic counterterrorism operations. Forces like France's *Gendarmerie*, Italy's *Carabinieri*, and Spain's *Guardia Civil* represent force models that, in many respects, are nearly ideal for HLS missions: highly mobile, well-armed and equipped and, perhaps most importantly, well versed in law enforcement and public security roles. These forces are also quite numerous: in some instances, notably in France and Italy, they rival the active army force in size.[33] In many cases, these paramilitary forces, while nominally part of the ministry of defense, work on a daily basis with the ministries of the interior and justice in carrying out general law enforcement functions, which typically account for nearly three-quarters of their efforts. Thus, they are well informed of the local security situation on a daily basis and can often detect changes in that status, producing the kind of intelligence so useful in HLS missions.

In addition to these paramilitary police forces, there are also several kinds of police forces that also carry out HLS tasks. Unlike the US, several European countries have national police forces, in addition to municipal and local police forces. Often, these national police forces, such as Austria's *Gendarmerie,* have small, highly specialized units that are responsible for domestic counterterrorism operations.[34] There is also a range of special police forces to be found in many countries, whose tasks include HLS functions. Representative of these special police forces are the French *Compagnies Républicaines de Sécurité* (CRS), Italy's *Guardia di Finanza,* and Germany's *Bundesgrenzschutz.* The CRS functions as the principal reserve of the national police force, and is frequently employed in special event security tasks and critical infrastructure protection. Others, like the *Guardia di Finanza,* have HLS tasks in addition to their primary function of reinforcing border security efforts. The *Bundesgrenzschutz's* famous *Grenzschutzgruppe 9* (GSG9) is the principal counterterrorism unit in Germany.[35]

The US has few of these kinds of forces, and must rely on state and local law enforcement assets to carry out many of these missions. The restrictions on the use of federal military forces in law enforcement are extremely circumscribed. For example, active US Army units are prohibited by the *Posse Comitatus* Act of 1878, still in effect, from

33. French Gendarmerie web site, www.defense.gouv.fr/gendarermie; Italian Carabinieri web site, www.carabinieri.it/Arma; Spanish Guardia Civil web site, www.guardiacivil.org.

34. Austrian Gendarmerie web site, www.gendarmerie.at.n The Austrian Army provides considerable support for Austrian border security forces.

35. French CRS web site, www.interieur.gouv.fr/rubriques/c/c3; Italian Guardia di Finanza web site, www.gdf.it/, German Bundesgrenzschutz web site, www.bundesgrenzschutz.de.

carrying out law enforcement functions.[36] As a consequence, leaders must often rely on reserve forces, such as the National Guard, to provide HLS forces *in extremis*.

Moreover, despite the establishment of the DHS, there is little appetite for establishing a national police force. Many Americans would view such a force sceptically as a major expansion of the power of the federal government. This, compounded by the concerns raised by the expanded federal law enforcement functions established by legislation such as the Patriot Act, make it unlikely that there will be a future increase in the federal government's law enforcement abilities, despite the obvious advantages that accrue to the struggle against soft security threats from such initiatives.[37]

## HOMELAND SECURITY AND SOFT SECURITY: A BLIND SPOT?

September 11, 2001, forced the US to take notice of terrorism. But it also forced the US to recognize that it is also threatened by a broad range of soft security threats, many of which support terrorist activities. The United States is grappling with the huge challenge of adapting its policies and institutions to deal with the threat of catastrophic terrorism, as represent by the Al-Qaeda threat. It is not alone in this task. European countries have faced a variety of terror threats over the past decades and have developed a range of responses to them. Like the US, they now face the possibility of catastrophic acts of terrorism, and must adapt the institutions and polices developed for earlier terror threats to these new ones.

Whilst the apparent single-minded focus of the US on the threat of catastrophic terrorism might lead one to conclude that this has created a blind spot for other soft security concerns, careful analysis reveals that this is not the case. Increased attention to combating terrorism has also meant increased attention to other threats. This

36. The *Posse Comitatus* Act of 1878 prohibits active military units of the Army and Air Force from acting in a law enforcement role except in cases of extreme national emergency, as declared by the President. See www.dojgov.net/posse_comitatus_act/htm.
37. For more information on the Patriot Act, see www.aclu.org.

heightened level of vigilance brings with it a more comprehensive approach to combating soft security threats.

However, significant obstacles remain. Preparing for catastrophic terrorist events is not the top priority for most European governments, and many still lack the necessary legislative basis for countering this threat. Their continuing focus on the range of less significant, in the American view, soft security threats and other less threatening national terror threats makes them somewhat out of sync with US priorities. The US does, however, recognise that these efforts can reveal significant intelligence that can be of great use in the US's global effort against terror. Likewise, additional attention to sources of terrorist financing in the US, such as that supporting the IRA, has helped European counterterrorism efforts.

The institutionalization of the US effort in the Department of Homeland Security is without doubt a major step forward, and has created the opportunity for increased cooperation and sharing of key intelligence. The establishment of a major interlocutor for a significant range of soft security concerns will make these efforts easier, if still a long way from seamless. The fact that there are still many other players, such as the departments of justice and commerce, in the soft security enforcement effort makes coordination with multiple partners still necessary.

There is a clear understanding that close cooperation with friends and allies across the soft security spectrum is essential because of the often-symbiotic relationship between criminals and terrorists. While the attention of the US may be increased to the extent that this cooperation can be linked to the fight against terrorism, it obviously has spillover effects in other areas as well. Just as the war on terrorism cannot be won single-handedly, so too must the struggle against soft security concerns be conducted on a cooperative basis. This will require increased cooperation, to include intelligence sharing, as well as the development of new relationships, established on the basis of mutual trust and confidence. As the US goes through the birthing pains of establishing the Department of Homeland Security, this will not be easy, but it will be essential. The US is now awake to the dangers represented by other soft threats, and this alertness must be capitalized on—or the opportunity will be lost.

# SOFT SECURITY THREATS IN THE NEW EUROPE: THE CASE OF THE BALKAN REGION

FOTIOS MOUSTAKIS

'You cannot have a process where Balkan countries pretend to reform and we pretend to believe them.'

Chris Patten, EU Commissioner in charge of External Relations
BBC World News, 25 November, 2002

## SECURITY: A GENERAL PERSPECTIVE

Although security has always been a central concept in international relations, it was not always properly defined by scholars in the field.[1] Arnold Wolfers was one of the few academics who attempted to define the meaning of the term security which is now regarded as

1. Brock, P. and Berkowitz, M. 'The Emerging Field of National Security', *World Politics*, Vol. 19, 1966, p. 124.

"standard."[2] There is a general acceptance that it implies freedom from threats to core values, but there is disagreement about what those values should be. There is also disagreement about whether the focus for security should be at the level of the individual, the state, or the international community.

From 1945 to the late 1980s security was interpreted in a rather rigid and narrow sense to mean simply the military security of the state, that is, almost synonymous with military power. According to this simplistic logic the more military power, or the more favourable the military balance, the more security. Similarly, the variety of potential threats tended in practice to be reduced simply to external military threats. To this end the protection of the people within states was the prime responsibility of the state, and not an issue of international concern.

However, the dynamics of European security have become considerably more difficult to comprehend in recent years. First an "amorphous threat-free post Cold War security setting"[3] has replaced the distinct Alliance-wide threat from the Soviet Union.

2. Wolfers, Arnold: 'National Security as an Ambiguous Symbol', in idem: *Discord and Collaboration. Essays on International Politics* (Baltimore: Johns Hopkins University Press, 1962), pp. 147–165 (quote from p. 150). See also Krell, Gert: 'The Development of the Concept of Security', in Jahn, Egbert & Sakamoto, Yoshikazu (eds): *Elements of World Instability: Armaments, Communication, Food, International Division of Labour*, Proceedings of the International Peace Research Association Eighth General Conference (Frankfurt: Campus Verlag, 1981), pp. 238–254; Jahn, Egbert: 'From International Peace Research to National Security Research', in Jaap, Nobel (ed.): *The Coming of Age of Peace Research. Studies in the Development of a Discipline* (Groningen: Styx, 1991), pp. 57–75; Frei, Daniel: 'Was ist unter Frieden und Sicherheit zu verstehen?', in Heisenberg, Wolfgang & Lutz, Dieter S. (eds) *Sicherheitspolitik Kontrovers. Frieden und Sicherheit. Status quo in Westeuropa und Wandel in Osteuropa* (Bonn: Bundeszentrale für politische Bildung 1990), Vol. 1, pp. 41–49; Stephenson, Carolyn: 'New Conceptions of Security and Their Implications for Means and Methods', in Tehranian, Katharine and Majid (eds): *Restructuring for World Peace. On the Threshold of the Twenty-First Century* (Creskil, NJ: Hampton Press 1992), pp. 47–61; Fischer, Dietrich: *Nonmilitary Aspects of Security. A Systems Approach* (Aldershot: Dartmouth and UNIDIR 1993). See also Møller, Bjørn: 'Security Concepts: New Challenges and Risks', *Working Papers*, No. 18 (Copenhagen: Centre for Peace and Conflict Research, 1993).

3. Tanner, Fred 'Conflict Management and European Security: The Problem of Collective Solidarity' Seminar in Leukerbad, Switzerland, 21/22 August 1998, http://www.isn. ethz.ch/securityforum/Online_Publications/WS4/Tanner.htm

Second, new risks and threats (the so-called "soft security threats") have increasingly affected European security from regions immediately adjoining Western Europe, such as the Balkans.

At this point it would be constructive to distinguish between hard and soft security. Hard security has traditionally "referred to the military defence of the state, seeing security issues in terms of the military balance as well as military strategy and tactics."[4] Soft security[5] refers to the non-military combat aspects of security. In other words it focuses on political, social, and economic concerns, such as poverty and unemployment, population explosion and environmental degradation, resurgent nationalism and social tensions, uncontrolled migration and coerced displacement, and the proliferation of narcotics, crime, and small arms.

Southeastern Europe represents for Europe a significant geostrategic and geopolitical region whose stability and security directly affects Europe's political and security infrastructure. Conflicts and notorious instability still loom in the Balkans[6] and, as a consequence, security cooperation in Europe currently struggles to cope with these risks of a non-military nature and ambiguous threat scenarios from "out-of-area." It is widely accepted that at the dawn of the 21st century the EU has not so far successfully addressed the Balkans' security deficiencies.

This article initially provides a generic picture of the Balkans and the hard security challenges currently at work. It will also identify the main forms of new security threats that are currently present in the region and explicate how these threats would be influenced by EU membership. It will outline the cooperative security measures

4. Archer, Clive 'Aspects of Soft Security', in Ojanen, Hanna (ed.), *The Northern Dimension: Fuel for the EU?*, (Helsinki: + UPI&IEP, program on the Northern Dimension of the CFSP), pp. 188–208.

5. In 1996 Niels Helveg Petersen, then Danish Foreign Minister, referred to the concept in the context of regional cooperation in Europe and mentioned "the so-called soft security risks . . . political and economic instability, ethnic conflict, minority problems, border disputes, the influx of refugees, trans-border environmental problems, and organized criminality." He saw the EU in itself as being one of the most successful examples of soft security policy, by demonstrating that "peace through integration" works.

6. For the purpose of this article the terms Balkans and South-Eastern Europe will be used interchangeably.

adopted by the Southeastern European countries and it will conclude by providing some thoughts on the future developments in the region influenced by current international developments, that is, the Bush doctrine and continuous transatlantic rift.

## THE BALKAN REGION: PAST AND PRESENT

At the beginning of the 20th century the security situation in the Balkans was marked by the disintegration of the Ottoman Empire, with the major European powers and the tiny Balkan states vying for its legacy. At the end of the 20th century the security situation in the Balkans was marked by the disintegration of Yugoslavia, with the former republics clashing over its legacy and the major powers over new spheres of influence in the region. Between these two events there stretched a whole century in which the powder keg became a metaphor for the Balkans, for the confrontations between the major European and world powers over spheres of interest and for the wars between Balkan states for disputed territories and the realisation of conflicting national programs.[7] Neither several Balkan wars, including the latest one in the territory of Yugoslavia, nor the two world wars have pacified Balkan soil.[8] On the contrary, they have provided strong evidence that there is a very long road to peace and stability in the Balkans.

Of course there are several reasons that contributed to the creation of the Balkans as a "powerful generator of instability in Europe,"[9] such as the geo-strategic and geo-political significance of the region for the big powers. The geo-strategic importance of the Balkans is based on two central facts. Firstly, the area lies astride important land routes between Europe and the Middle East. In recent years the Balkans have been plagued by intra-state conflicts

7. For a comprehensive study of the Balkan region and the influence of the major European powers see Glenny, Misha *The Balkans 1804–1999*, (London: Granta 1999).

8. However, the period of Soviet domination during the Cold War era did pacify the region.

9. Interview with Professor P. Simic, Director of the Institute of International Politics and Economics, Belgrade, during a Corfu International Conference about Conflict Resolution, summer 1997.

and threats from failed states and non-state actors. As Ognian Shentov, the chairman of the Center for the Study of Democracy emphasized, "The border line between external and internal security has become even more blurred. Geographic remoteness and geopolitical advantages which characterized and shaped the Balkans no longer provide a safe haven."[10] *Au contraire*, international crime syndicates have nurtured a fusion between criminalised political and economic elites and as a result organized crime threatens to overwhelm law enforcement resources as well as business transactions and trade. Cyber crime has also become a common occurrence, while corruption has turned into a strategic threat to established as well as new democracies.

Secondly, the Balkan territory, between the Danube river, the Black Sea, and the Mediterranean, represents a significant factor in the European and global strategy of the major powers. The Balkans had its greatest geopolitical significance in the early decades of the last century. In the Second World War, the geo-strategic significance of the Balkans declined from the standpoints of Germany's main thrusts of expansion and also the strategic preoccupation of the big allied powers. Although after the Second World War the so-called Iron Curtain cut the Balkans in two, decisions about the development and outcome of the Cold War were taken far from the Balkans. Yet neither bloc would give up the Balkans, even though they did not look upon it as a region of essential importance.[11]

This decline in the geo-strategic significance of the Balkans might have continued after the eastern bloc collapsed. Even if a crisis had not emerged in the Balkans, against the background of the break-up of the Yugoslav federation, the Balkan area has increasingly lagged behind the tempo of European integration. The Balkans are now in

10. Ognian Shentov, *Shaping a Common Security Agenda for South East Europe*, paper delivered at an international conference, Sofia, September 5–6, 2003.

11. "During the Cold War, the balance of the Balkans was regulated within the broader European balance under the '2+2+2' formula. Two of the six Balkan states were members of NATO (Greece and Turkey), two were members of the Warsaw Treaty (Romania and Bulgaria), and Yugoslavia was non-aligned from the mid-1950s, while Albania was in self-imposed isolation from the end of the 1950s. Although not a single ethnic ethnic or territorial problem that was prevalent in the Balkans was resolved in the course of this Cold War period, the region was calm because the bipolar division helped suppress the many local disputes that were threatening to burst." Interview with P. Simic, Corfu, 1997.

the limelight for the following reasons. First, the crisis in the former Yugoslavia and the current challenges to human, inter-group, national, and regional security in the Balkans reflect negatively on the process of European integration and the establishment of a security community. Second, that crisis has in some respects confirmed that the big European and world powers share common interests, but has also highlighted their differences of approach and interests, based on old historical and geo-strategic beliefs. Third, rightly or wrongly, attempts to address the security deficiencies in the former Yugoslav space and the Balkans as a whole were seen as putting to the test the ability of the European and international community to control and address successfully crises and threats in the post-Cold War period. It is for these reasons that the Balkans are today again at the center of European and American attention and will most probably remain so as long as security deficiencies in this region remain unresolved.

## NEW SECURITY CHALLENGES IN THE BALKANS: PROSPECTS FOR EU-NATO INTEGRATION

It is widely acknowledged that eventual Balkan integration into the EU will probably be the most important political event in Southern Europe and Europe as a whole. It will have a tremendous effect on these countries as well as on the EU. Currently, the applicant states and the EU are focusing their attention on the Copenhagen criteria (the creation of a functioning constitutional state with a competitive market economy) and the adoption and implementation by the applicant states of the *acquis communautaire* (a complete set of common regulations and norms). However, little public attention is devoted to soft security issues and their impact on the new EU external borders once the Balkan states are fully integrated into the EU structure.

Girard Stoudmann, Director of OSCE office for Democratic Institutions and Human Rights, has identified the main challenges for the EU and the Balkan states as:

1. Implementing the Schengen regime
2. Preventing and combating trafficking in drugs and human beings, fighting organized crime and corruption

3. Civilian control
4. Integrating multicultural values.[12]

The migration problem and the integration of many foreigners and displaced persons entering Europe demand harmonization of the asylum, visa, and migration procedures. Schengen will be in danger of losing all credibility if the controls at the external borders are not efficient: border guards therefore have to be adequately equipped, structured and trained. We already witness at the Greek-Turkish borders the enormous difficulties of adopting the Schengen regime, where Greek authorities try, in most cases unsuccessfully, to stem the incessant and rising numbers of illegal immigrants from Asia. Inter-European cooperation and coordination is essential for the successful implementation of this regime.

The issues of combating trafficking in drugs and human beings and fighting organized crime and corruption are considered more and more as new threats to international security since the transnational crime infrastructure also benefits terrorism. The risks involved in increasingly sophisticated criminal networks and their links with political extremism constitute an unwelcome development of the last decade. It is widely accepted that the international community has paid little attention to the new ways in which organized crime, and especially transnational economic crime, has evolved. In the Balkans, quite often, nationalist and even patriotic rhetoric serves to disguise criminal economic interests. The magnitude of the problem was highlighted in the recent assassination of the Serbian Prime Minster Djindjic by powerful criminal elements. Corruption-free border guards and security forces are a pre-condition to addressing this challenge successfully.

Security and armed forces (police, border guards, militia, and other law enforcement bodies plus the military) play a vital role in the attempt to deal effectively with soft security threats and it is imperative that they remain under civilian control. Balkan parliaments have to further develop these control mechanisms, to ensure that the behavior of security forces is fully in line with international human rights standards, while the professionalism and efficiency of

---

12. Presentation by Girard Stoudmann, *European Integration and its impact on the Security Sector of the Applicant States*, at ISF Conference, Zurich, 14–16 October 2002.

these forces needs to be further strengthened. Efficient internal oversight of these forces is also needed to ensure accountability and proper conduct.

With regard to the integration of multicultural values, the Balkan states will need to integrate linguistic and ethnic minorities, in order to create security forces fully reflecting the reality of a democratic civil society. This process, of course, can only be implemented parallel to the integration of minorities at the state level, a step that has already been taken by some countries such as FYROM (Former Yugoslav Republic of Macedonia) and Bosnia. It is important for the Balkan states to acknowledge that any sensible security policy will consider the minority factor as key to long-term internal stability and security.

It is true that the EU security concept is currently evolving from a rather narrow one containing mainly a politico-military dimension to something broader and more comprehensive, such as the one advocated by the OSCE. The OSCE concept of comprehensive security links military, economic, and human dimensions together as all equally relevant for peace and stability. Security and respect for human rights are closely linked. Long-term stability and security, economic development, and the building of democratic institutions guaranteeing fundamental freedoms and respect for human rights are interconnected and interdependent.

The southeastern European countries are not dealing with these diverse and multiple challenges alone, and the OSCE is not the only organization that has attempted to address these issues. They have been supported by a multitude of mechanisms and initiatives driven by international, European, and Euro-Atlantic organizations, especially NATO and the European Union. One of these initiatives, for example, is the NATO-led peacekeeping operation in Bosnia-Herzegovina (SFOR) and another in Kosovo (KFOR). The thousands of military personnel who make up these missions are proof of the international community's commitment to maintaining peace and security in Southeastern Europe.

With the support of their Western partners, the countries of the region have also started a process to build regional structures of cooperation that could be used to cope with current risks. These cooperative structures include the Southeastern European Defense Ministerial (SEEDM), the Southeastern European Cooperation

Process (SEECP), and the Southeastern European Cooperative Initiative and Multinational Peace Force in Southeastern Europe (SEEBRIG). A particular achievement in this framework is the Regional SECI Center for Combating Trans-Border Criminality, hosted by Romania in Bucharest. This is perhaps the most significant initiative from the region aimed at fighting drugs, arms, human trafficking, and illegal immigration.

The most inclusive international community involvement in the region is the establishment of the Stability Pact, a comprehensive set of initiatives in the most critical fields of stability and security.[13] Though there has been criticism of the pace of activities as well as the total amount of resources involved in the process, no one can deny the value of the process as a whole, which encourages regional cooperation and provides the Balkan countries with the necessary tools and instruments to address military and non-military security threats.[14]

The Yugoslav conflicts have not only revealed the impact of instability on the rest of the European continent, but also highlighted the interdependence of both "hard" (military) and "soft" (nonmilitary) security. It has become clear to all that

> "a long term co-ordinated and coherent international presence, the core part of which will be European, will therefore be needed to implement change and transition through combined means, encompassing the whole spectrum of conflict prevention and crisis management mechanisms."[15]

---

13. It is instructive to mention the Stability Pact, since it aims not only at strengthening countries in South Eastern Europe in their efforts to foster peace, democracy, and respect for human rights and economic prosperity, in order to achieve stability in the whole region. It also promotes unimpeded contacts among citizens, combating organized crime, corruption, and terrorism and all criminal and illegal activities.

14. For Daniel N. Nelson, the Stability Pact is "not what we or the Balkans needed. It is diplomatic Prozac at a time when shock therapy is required. It offers inducements and rewards before the heavy lifting. It suggests that we can buy and educate the Balkans towards market democracy in the long term, before a secure milieu exists in which to nurture such fragile institutions." *The Southeast Europe Stability Pact: Stability Without Security Is Bad for the Balkans*, speech at European Studies Discussion, The Woodrow Wilson Center, Washington, DC, 20 October 1999.

15. Clement, Sophia, *The Balkans and Beyond: The European Perspective on Future Regional Stability*, in East European Studies Special reports, available at http:/wwics.si.edu/ees/special/2000/clemen.pdf.

## SOFT SECURITY THREATS IN THE BALKANS

The primary lesson we should take from the Balkans is that it requires time, resources, and commitment to help countries rebuild themselves. It is widely accepted that one important transformation is occurring in the Balkans today. This is the transition away from nationalism, dictatorship, and war towards peace, democracy, and a European future. However, the process of European integration for all of the Balkans cannot be completed if soft security threats are still present in the region.

The issue that needs to be considered is that except for sporadic media interest, the international community has paid little attention to the new ways in which organized crime and, especially, transnational economic crime, have evolved. Corruption, as a way of soliciting government "cooperation," has become a major risk to national as well as international security. The involvement in organized crime of institutions and individuals from the security sector is evidence that society's ability to protect itself from the criminal world has been undermined. Particularly worrying and dangerous is the existence of established smuggling channels that are aided by corrupt individuals in the customs and law-enforcement agencies, or other state institutions. The importance of this type of systemic corruption can be highlighted by the following statistic: between 50 and 70 percent of the gross domestic product of the Balkan countries crosses their borders.[16] One can easily imagine the magnitude of the threat that corruption in border and custom controls poses to a nation's economy and security. In some cases even members of the armed forces are involved in trans-border smuggling activities. For example, in 2003, two cases that illustrated this point were the use of Bulgaria's Black Sea naval base in Atia for large-scale smuggling operations and the involvement of high-level Romanian military officers in cigarette smuggling through Romania's Otopeni international airport.

The economic foundation of organised crime is reinforced by two factors—the high unemployment rate and the enormous share of the "grey" economy. The 'grey' economy generates between 40

16. Ognian Shentov, *Shaping a Common Security Agenda for South East Europe*, International Conference, Sofia, September 5–6 2003, p. 2.

and 50 percent of the national income of the countries in Southeast Europe. The average unemployment for the region is 21%.[17] This is a huge human resource for organized crime groups. High unemployment also creates an environment that is conducive to the trafficking in human beings, which is one of the most profitable illegal activities in Europe.

The spread of economic crime contributes to the persistence of the grey and black sectors in the region's national economies. For many countries, these sectors account for 30 to 40% of their GDP.[18] According to some estimates, for countries such as Turkey, Albania, FYROM, and Serbia and Montenegro, the percentages are even higher. Just like the legal market, the grey and black economies are governed by the logic of demand and supply. The illegal trafficking towards Western Europe increases the risks to the security of the entire continent. The millions of people that participate in the grey economies in the Balkans are also a significant source of illegal workers in Western Europe. Illegal immigrants also form a natural setting not only for the spread of organized criminal groups but also of terrorist organisations.

According to UN and EU data, the Balkans play an increasing role in transborder crime. Once a transit territory for criminal groups, the Balkans is gradually becoming a launching pad for bandit activities, where the traffickers of humans, drugs, stolen vehicles, and cultural and historic valuables are based.

Illegal human trafficking through the Balkans is a thriving business.

> 'The Vienna-based UN Immigration Centre claims that some 10,000 white slaves are being illegally transferred from Eastern Europe westwards. The expansion of traffic channels, including consumer and industrial products, drugs and humans gave birth to a trend, previously unknown. According to the National Statistics Institute some 61.5% of the indicted dealers are in the age group of 14 to 29.'[19]

They are charged mainly with theft, but a growing number are indicted for document forgery and contraband. Contraband operations are characterized by a high degree of organisation. Customs

17. Petkan, Ilie, 'Corruption, Contraband And Institutional Reform', *PARI daily*, 3 February 2003.
18. Ibid.
19. Ibid.

officers are involved in criminal partnerships with businessmen, underground groups and their businesses, commercial structures with shadow activities, carriers, and individual importers. These are lasting partnerships, in which the customs officers receive both single commissions for occasional "services" and regular benefits in import operations. In some cases customs officers have succumbed to the pressure of local and central authority representatives, influential groups, and criminal organizations. The bribe is a percentage of the amount that the customs officer spares his clients and is determined primarily by the specific risk and the necessity to agree the legal offence with his bosses. Usually the bribe is some 30% of the amount of the levies and fees due. In some cases the officer receives, apart from the cash, a commission in-kind, or even long-term loans.[20]

One should not forget, though, the demand side. The trafficking of women and children is largely driven by the demand for their services. The drug trafficking trade is also driven and sustained by the growing number of drug users in Western Europe. In some EU countries cigarette smuggling is eased by the lack of efficient measures to stop it and by increasing demand for cheap cigarettes as a result of high tobacco taxes. Finally, the illegal labor market is also driven by the demand for cheap labor, from which employers in the West make a significant profit.

Despite the fact that the US has spent around $24 billion in the last decade for the reconstruction of the Balkans and the frequent meetings of all regional foreign ministers under the umbrella of the Southeast Europe Cooperation Process (SEECP), where they agreed to work together on key challenges facing the region including trade and the fight against organized crime, groups that traffic in persons, drugs, and weapons are well entrenched in the region and quite powerful.[21]

On 12 March 2003, Serbian Prime Minister Zoran Djindjic was assassinated in front of the Serbian government building by sniper, Zvezdan Jovanovic, Deputy Commander of the infamous paramilitary unit known as the Red Berets. Fortunately, rather than crumble, the Serbian government came together, elected Zoran Zivkovic as Djindjic's successor, imposed a state of emergency,

20. Ibid.

21. For more information about the problems of soft security threats in Bosnia see interview with Paddy Ashdown, BBC *Breakfast with Frost*, 14 January 2003.

began a far-reaching crackdown on organized crime, and instituted sweeping defence reforms. The assassination reinvigorated the stalled reform process in Serbia and revealed the nexus between organized crime and war crimes inductees and their supporters. The crackdown resulted in the arrest of more than 4500 people and effectively dismantled Serbia's largest organized crime syndicates, most notably the Zemun clan whose leaders were behind the Djindjic assassination.

It was only after the tragic death of the Serbian Prime Minister that Belgrade took significant steps to cooperate with the International Criminal Tribunal for the former Yugoslavia (ICTY). Following the assassination, authorities apprehended the remaining "Vukovar Three" indictees, Miroslav Radic and Veselin Sljivancanin. In addition, Serbian State Security Chief Jovica Stanisic, architect of the Serbian nationalist policy of ethnic cleansing, and his deputy Franko Simatovic, founder of the Red Berets, were apprehended and transferred to The Hague.[22]

In the light of the repercussions of this tragic event it is important for NATO and the EU to formulate a new security policy agenda that seeks to broaden the scope of NATO's responsibilities and improve its capacity to deal with soft security challenges (see Table I below).

No one could suggest that we have reached the end of problems in the Balkans. It is true that the prospects of large-scale conflict in the region are low, while democracy and pluralism are slowly taking root. However the pattern currently emerging in the Balkans shows that the world's attention to new security threats, even before 11 September 2001, continued to fall. Over the next two to three years, NATO and especially American troops are likely to reduce their peacekeeping presence further, foreign aid will decline, and international attention will continue to drift elsewhere (to the Middle East for example).[23]

---

22. For more information about the current situation in Serbia and Montenegro see Statement of Paul W. Jones, Acting Deputy Assistant Secretary for Europe and Eurasia, US Department of State, Hearing of the Senate Foreign Relations Committee, Sub-committee on Europe Successor States to Pre-1991 Yugoslavia, Progress and Challenges 25 June 2003.

23. See *The Economist*, 'Almost Like One Country', 27 September 2003, p. 44.

TABLE I
What do European Union Citizens Fear?

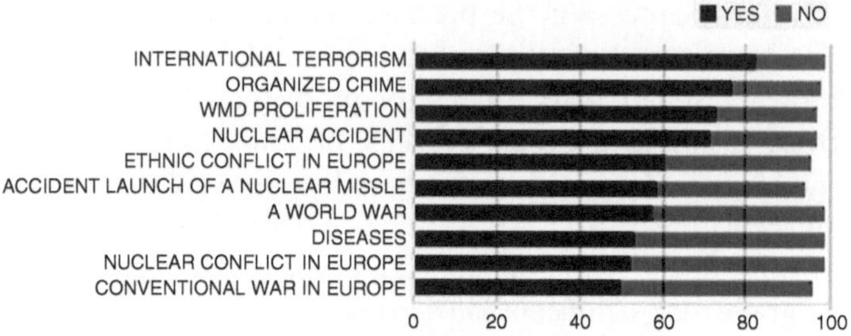


SOURCE: EUROBAROMETER, OCT/NOV 2002

The Bush administration has led the exodus, progressively turning over Balkans responsibilities—both long-term development and short-term crisis management—to the European Union. The EU, on one hand is acquiring greater responsibility for Balkan affairs, while on the other, it finds itself absorbed in internal debates over expansion, constitutional revision, and pressing global matters such as the ongoing conflicts in the Middle East. Although efforts at streamlining the EU's weaknesses in security and foreign policymaking are obvious, the strengthening European capabilities in these areas will take years. Thus, Brussels' ability to handle the assortment of challenges it has taken on in southeastern Europe, and Washington's willingness and ability to be an effective junior (but still prodding) partner, remain very much in doubt.

In the meantime the Balkan region is attempting to address a series of security-related issues, each with the capacity to spiral out of control again, in particular the future and security threats in Bosnia and Herzegovina, Kosovo, and FYROM. As Gareth Evans of International Crisis Control argued in his address on the Trilateral Commission on 11 November 2001:

> 'What is absolutely clear is that there are no short cuts to stability, least of all involving any major region-wide initiatives, as appealing as that course may seem. Everything we know about the states of mind of all the relevant parties, both inside and outside the region, tells us that an all-encompassing big-bang diplomatic conference to settle boundary and political issues once and for all is destined to remain quite out of reach for the foreseeable future. And so too is an all-encompassing big-bang process

like the negotiation of a Western Balkans free trade area, or a strategy for a joint accession process to the EU.'[24]

Even self-evidently attractive regional coordination mechanisms like the Stability Pact for South Eastern Europe have been struggling to add value to the cause of regional stability and economic advance. Partly this has been a product of inflated expectations—inevitably disappointed—about massive new resources flowing to the region. But the Pact process has also suffered from inadequate authority, confused priority setting and less than spectacular management.

When considering the need for innovative approaches to analysing the security risks and the conduct of an adequate security policy, one should emphasise the increasing role of non-state actors in both domestic and international politics. In Bulgaria, an example of this new role is *Coalition 2000*, an anticorruption initiative of a group of non-governmental organization working with the support of the United States Agency for International Development. The work of this coalition illustrates the advantages that public-private partnerships offer in countering soft security threats.

What about the current security situation in some of the Balkan states? There is nothing self-sustaining about Bosnia at the moment. If the international community walked away tomorrow all the institutions that have been built since 1995 would most probably crumble away. The Dayton accord made sense as a glorified armistice, but not as a comprehensive settlement holding the key to self-sustainable peace and stability. Its objective was clear—to stop the fighting and hold the country together—but the means by which that objective was to be secured were deeply flawed. Its constitutional machinery—with a central government having to wrestle with a structure deeply divided into two entities, three constitutive peoples, ten powerful cantons in one half of the country, and, effectively, three armies—is unworkable,[25] self-frustrating, and self-defeating, and not calculated to create any kind of viable economy of serious interest to foreign investors.

24. Evans, Gareth, *Advancing Balkan Stability*, address to the Trilateral Commission, 11 November 2001.

25. *The Economist* Survey: 'The Balkans', 24 January 1998, pp. 6–8.

With regard to Kosovo a very senior Brussels official stated: "We have two rules round the EU about Kosovo's final status. First, don't talk about it. Second, don't think about it."[26] Under UN Security Council Resolution 1244, the final status of Kosovo is completely undecided. The lawyers of the United Nations in New York pick over every move that UNMIK wants to make, to ensure that nothing is done by the international community that might be perceived as prejudicing the eventual decision on this matter. The most pressing internal reason for not delaying is that a whole range of issues essential for the building of a healthy, stable society in Kosovo cannot be effectively resolved without addressing the status question. UN lawyers are blocking the privatisation of formerly socially-owned enterprises in order not to risk prejudicing the final status. Serious investment is hampered as long as there is no clarity as to future jurisdiction. As a result, Kosovo's economic recovery is limited to street-level, import-related trading, and major economic assets are left to deteriorate.

With regard to Bulgaria, Albania, and Romania, it is widely acknowledged that state institutions have been significantly strengthened over the past three years with the adoption of several excellent laws. It can therefore be said that these countries are now in the implementation phase, where the challenge is to put these laws into practice. However, there remains a serious discrepancy between the laws as written and their enforcement. There are serious problems with the political independence of the judiciary, the professionalism of judges and prosecutors (basic salaries), and, above all, the corruption that eats at the heart of the justice system. The continued contribution of international institutions is crucial to the efforts being made to strengthen both state and government. Despite efforts, there is still no modern or well functioning public administration. This is due to a mentality which politicises everything and places party interests ahead of the state. Unfortunately populism is a major characteristic of Balkan politics.

Lastly, in FYROM the problem lies in the fact that the Slav-Macedonian majority did not wish to address the grievances of the Albanian minority. However, the international community intervened promptly and effectively. In August 2001, European and US envoys succeeded in brokering a political agreement between

26. Evans, op.cit.

Macedonian and ethnic Albanian leaders to introduce far-reaching, overdue and necessary constitutional and legal reforms. As a workable basis for a sustainable multi-ethnic democracy, the Framework Agreement is significant for the future of FYROM, since it addresses the soft security threats.

It is true that, as the high representative in Bosnia Paddy Ashdown stressed, Europe "has only one big carrot, EU membership, with which to influence Balkan behaviour."[27] Hence, the international community and especially the EU needs to play a pivotal role in helping local reformers to put their country irrevocably on the path to stability. To this end the international community must try to adopt some of the following measures:

- Provide clear incentives, including increased financial and technical assistance, to reformers to combat organised crime and corruption.
- Provide reformers with access to law enforcement specialists and intelligence sharing.
- Condition new and substantial economic assistance upon demonstrable progress in cleaning out corrupt and criminalized structures and putting transparent and democratic modes of governance in place.
- Institute clear codes of conduct and financial disclosure statements for all elected officials, election candidates, political parties, and military officials.
- Enforce civilian control over all the security forces, including paramilitary structures outside the regular army.
- Stop encouraging nationalist diehards to believe that they have a future outside current political structures.
- Remove the mechanisms for state control of the media and cease harassment of independent journalists.
- Carry out complete lustration of the judiciary, coupled with a process of general reappointment.[28]

27. Abramowitz, Morton & Hurlburt, Heather 'Can the EU Hack the Balkans', *Foreign Affairs* September/October 2002, //www.b92.net/feedback/misljenja/abramowitz/index.php

28. Some of these measures have been recommended to combat soft security threats in Serbia & Montenegro by the International Crisis Group. See *Serbia After Djindjic*, 13 March 2003, http://www.intl-crisis-group.org/projects/showreport.cfm?reportid=921.

## CONCLUSIONS

With the increasing military, economic, and civil intervention of the international community, we are witnessing a shift from hard to soft security risks. The extensive nature of these threats to stability in the region requires a comprehensive and trans-regional response. Probably the greatest success of NATO in the Kosovo crisis was the prevention of a destabilization of the region as a whole. The soft security risks are a more intrinsically EU matter than are military and defense issues. These soft risks are also closely related to the imminence and proximity of EU eastern enlargement. It is widely believed that the survival of the Balkan states is largely due to European reform assistance. Overall, the distinct tendency is for ethnic risks to become economic risks in weak states along the EU border. The main soft security risks originate from socio-economic uncertainty and unemployment, a high level of corruption in the political and economic systems, a low level of trust in the police and judiciary, a limited capacity to absorb international assistance effectively as well as from organized crime, which is related to deficits in law enforcement, border controls, and customs: smuggling, drug trafficking, trafficking in human beings, and other activities.

On the whole, the region's stability and its ability to build institutions that can deal with hard and soft security threats depend on how and when it answers crucial existential questions. What will be the structure and political orientation of Serbia, Montenegro, and Kosovo? How successfully will FYROM address the grievances of the ethnic Albanian minority? How can Bosnia achieve some economic dynamism and stable political security? These and many other questions highlight crucial considerations for the establishment of secure self-government, for fostering justice and reconciliation, and for promoting longer-term social progress across the region. To reach a mutually sustainable and acceptable solution will require a political course beyond what is envisaged in the Stabilization and Association Process or Stability Pact. The carrot of EU membership will start to seem less tempting if the EU cannot make the prospect of membership realistic and the benefits tangible. It is high time for the EU to take the lead and to lead responsibly. The stakes are high.

# STRENGTHENING "SOFT" SECURITY: WHAT IS TO BE DONE?

JAMES SHERR

The principal source of soft security problems is not weak international mechanisms, but weak and ineffective states. My role in this article is, first, to discuss this uncomfortable truth and its implications, which are serious. Differences in political orders, business cultures, and law enforcement and security systems are creating new dividing lines in Europe, and the policies of the European Union and the Russian Federation are now deepening and formalizing that divide.

A question immediately arises. How can anyone possibly call Russia or Ukraine weak states? Their state structures are highly developed, possibly even over-developed. By some calculations, the number of government employees, particularly at regional and local level, is greater than it was during the Soviet period. Those who work inside executive structures in Moscow and Kiev are for the most part highly educated and many of them are very expert and professional in the work they do. The foreign visitor crossing a border, the investor seeking an investment opportunity, the ordinary Russian or Ukrainian citizen certainly does not feel that these states are weak. But the people *we* are concerned with—the black market business people, the supplier of contraband, the arms merchant, money launderer, and human trafficker—often do. What is more, many of these people feel that the state is their silent partner. Since this is true of the region's "strongest" post-Communist states, it makes sense to focus on them, because in doing so, we will underscore the problems faced by others.

## THE SOURCE OF THE PROBLEM

To rephrase an old morsel of wisdom, "nothing is more important or more difficult to discover than the pedigree of ideas." So it is with institutions and their practices. The pedigree of the problem of "soft security threats" lies in the illicit continuities between Communism and post-Communism. Most people know little about these continuities. Many who do know prefer to ignore them. We should not. Let us cite three:

First, the Communist ("socialist") political order denied legitimacy to virtually all private enterprise, but in practice private enterprise and intermediaries between the legal and illegal economies were essential to the functioning of the "system." Shadowy individuals and, in time, "shadow structures" became well connected with local governments and, progressively, central governments too. Because their activity was criminal, their mentality was criminal, and it still is.

Second, the collapse of this system reversed the roles of authority and accomplice. The destruction of the old system of authority legalised nearly everything that had been illegal before. As a result, new capital and its allies in new state structures proceeded to privatize nearly everything in sight—a process which, *de facto*, included creeping privatization of public authorities and the state itself. Before Boris Yeltsin and Leonid Kuchma shut them down, anti-corruption commissions provided abundant evidence of these trends. The style of this newly privatized business reflected its totalitarian, undemocratic, and criminal roots. Wealth creation became predatory rather than entrepreneurial. Economies became, indeed remained, producer- rather than consumer-oriented. Methods of business, like earlier methods of administration, remained inbred, collusive, and opaque. Networks rather than markets drove economic activity. As a result of all these factors, many ordinary people continued to equate business with immorality, as they did under socialism—now with good reason, because in this Darwinian environment very few have treated business as a transaction designed to benefit both buyer and seller.

Third, the collapse of state budgets has proved to be even more important than the collapse of the Soviet Union. In this context, the old Soviet curse, "may you live on your salary," has acquired an obvious importance. Bureaucracies have become rent-seeking entities for the sake of survival. Yet the obvious remedy—"better fewer, but better" (and better paid)—has been ignored. Thanks to their private entrepreneurship, bureaucracies have grown in size. In turn, the legal order has become more complex, justifying more bureaucrats and more regulation. Official security structures have also proliferated. In the Russian Federation, 14 state security structures—not branches or departments, but separate ministries, services, agencies, and committees—had come into existence by 1995, each of them with its own component of troops. A similar development took place in Ukraine. If the state cannot finance these structures, is it not obvious that somebody else will?

These developments are not only mutually reinforcing. They have plunged society into vicious cycles that seem almost impossible to break. What causes black markets and crime? The absence of an attractive white (legal) economy. What makes the white economy attractive? Incentives and security. Who provides security? The state. Who provides finance for the state? Taxpayers in the white economy.

These supposedly economic and social problems are the major generator of soft security threats: threats which Ukraine's first (1997) National Security Concept rightly attributed to the weakness of state and society and the strength of those who would undermine both. Since 1997 many positive trends have emerged alongside the negative ones. The fact remains that in much of East-Central Europe, the right people are weak and the wrong people are strong. This imbalance gives point to the Russian and Ukrainian distinction between a country's *nezavisimost'/nezalezhnist'* ("independence") and its *samostoyatel'nost'/samostiynist'* (its "ability to stand"). Unless the state is properly financed, it will not have this ability. But finance cannot solve the problem by itself. To what ends should finance be directed? And by what means?

## CIVIC STATES, WEAK STATES, AND PATHOLOGICAL STATES

The end must be the establishment of a state which is both legitimate and effective. That much is obvious. Less obvious is the fact that unless legitimacy and effectiveness *both* exist, neither will exist. Effectiveness does not depend upon "powers," even if they are properly financed; it depends upon the powers being trusted by those they are meant to protect. When, as in Ukraine in early 2000, 20 percent of the population trust the security services and fewer than 12 percent trust the police and the courts, more power will not produce more effectiveness, just more of the same.[1] For its part, legitimacy does not depend upon a national or state "idea," because ideas will not protect people in their daily lives. For this, a country requires institutions: competent ones, motivated by an ethos of professionalism and furnished with the tools to act within the spheres entrusted to them. In sum, alongside the development of civil society, efforts must be made to develop a civic state. Today these efforts are hindered not only by the obvious factors of insolvency, incompetence and inertia, but by a number of serious misunderstandings. Chief among these is the belief that the democratization of state structures will weaken, rather than strengthen their ability to do their jobs. In at least three areas, democratization and effectiveness are inseparable:

*Accountability*

If military policy is simply the brainchild of a head of state, rather than the outcome of broad deliberation by executive structures and independent experts, how good can it possibly be? If the supervision and monitoring of force structures is not entrusted to elected institutions, but to an individual person—democratically elected or not—will a country be able (*pace* Leonid Kuchma) "to pull together at a crucial moment"?

*Transparency*

In their respective attitudes towards transparency we find one of the greatest differences between post-Communist and liberal democratic states. In the post-Communist, as in the Communist world, information still tends to be seen as a strategic commodity. In the liberal democratic world, it is seen as a public good, as vital to the health of the state and economy as blood circulation is to the body. So long as these distinctions exist, economic systems will remain distinct.

1. *National Security and Defence*, No 11, 2000 (Kiev: Ukrainian Centre for Economic and Political Studies), p. 10.

Transparency implies knowledge of what decisions are made, where they are made, by whom they are made, and why. The inability to know these things leads, at best, to confusion, duplication of effort and loss of money. At worst, it leads to illegality, threats to national security and conflict. It takes very little time for *bor'ba za informatsiyu*, the struggle for information, to become *informatsionnaya bor'ba*, the struggle to control and manipulate information for economic or political gain. Who gains when one of the largest corporations in the world, United Energy Systems of Russia, has no budget (as Anatoliy Chubays discovered when he became its chairman)? Without a budget, how is it possible to know who is making money, who is losing money, who is wasting money, and who is stealing it? Who gains and who loses when the owners and shareholders of energy production and distribution companies are concealed? How is it even possible to know who owns what—or who owes what to whom—in a Russian-Ukrainian energy "market" characterized by arbitrary price levels, hidden payment mechanisms, invisible partners, front companies, tax fraud, and an extensive barter trade? In many Central and Eastern European countries, the unfortunate truth is that transparency is often absent just where it is most needed.

### *Delegation of Authority*

The classic Soviet approach to the inertia and opacity of institutions—and the intrigues within them—has now been revived by President Putin: "strengthening the administrative vertical." This may strengthen the subordination of institutions, but it does nothing to strengthen *horizontal integration* inside them. For this, delegation of authority is needed. Without authority, officials will not assume responsibility. Often, they will not even take decisions. They will wait for orders, and once orders are given, they will wait for orders about how to implement the orders. This not only explains why, to this day, many post-Soviet administrative institutions are considerably larger than their Western counterparts (at an enormous real or hidden cost). It explains why people inside these institutions tend to work very hard and do very little.

The administrative culture in most NATO countries does not always diverge sufficiently from this pattern, and it can be criticized, even satirized, on many fronts. Yet relatively speaking at least, Western practices tend to be far more efficient. To take one example, inside NATO Headquarters, much policy is initiated and much of it made at mid level by committees: committees that are civil-military and interdepartmental in composition, with access to all information relevant to their responsibilities. Similar working practices exist in a number of Whitehall ministries. These practices result in a clear relationship between ideas from below and directives from above. They help to break down departmental barriers and knit institutions together. They also help to ensure that decisions are implemented swiftly and intelligently, because subordinates have participated in the process and therefore have enough information to know what they are doing and why.

What is the future for a country that allows post-Soviet practices and their analogues—"shadow structures," "subjective interests," and "financial-informational struggle"—to go unchecked? The consequences are plain to see in the former Soviet Union's four unrecognized political entities: the Pridnestrovian Moldovan Republic, the Republic of Abkhazia, the Republic of South Osetia, and the Nagorno-Karabakh Republic. In these entities the merger between business, crime, security services, and state structures is complete. Whereas the more limited connections between these spheres constitute a source of weakness in Russia, Ukraine, Moldova, Armenia, Azerbaijan, and Georgia, for these entities this merger is the source of their strength. For this reason, unrecognized states like Pridnestrov'ye can fairly be described as pathological states. Yet these pathologies are not simply a local problem. They feed on the state and civic weaknesses of their neighbors, as much as a parasite feeds on an unhealthy host. The containment and eventual eradication of these entities depends on the strengthening of state and society in neighboring states. If this does not happen, the pathologies will spread. If there is any doubt that democracy is relevant to security, one need only look at Pridnestrov'ye. Perhaps it is time for its neighbors to do so with open eyes. But it is also time that the European Union did so as well.

## THE INTERNATIONAL FACTOR

By enlarging NATO and the European Union, the member states of these bodies enlarged their definition of the West, as well as their commitments, interests, and vulnerabilities. This combination of ambition and vulnerability has infused enlargement with two impulses: integration and exclusion—or, to use a Cold War term, "containment." The European Union, to be sure, is committed to enlarge the European Economic Area. But it is even more determined to maintain the integrity of this area and protect the institutions and practices that make up the Single Market. This market is defined not only by a compatibility of political and economic systems, but of political and economic cultures.

The EU's *acquis communautaire*—whose documents now stretch to approximately 100,000 pages—is an absurdly and possibly insanely complex way of codifying what cannot be codified: a culture of civic mindedness, accountability, judicial integrity, transparency, entrepreneurship, openness, and business. For this reason, the EU is not fundamentally interested in the foreign policies of its neighbors and candidates. It is interested in their internal policies, and it judges these not by declarations and programmes but by how institutions behave in practice. The same has become true of NATO, as its focus has broadened beyond "deterrence and defense" to the strengthening of security against unconventional (soft security) threats. For both institutions, compatibility and effectiveness in the law enforcement and security realms are vital, and both institutions are convinced that without wider economic and political reform, reforms in these spheres will fail.

Understandable, even necessary, as these approaches are, the European Union has shied away from a vital question. Does it wish to be a magnet or a barrier? The case for barriers against illegal migration, organized crime, arms, and drugs is unanswerable. But must this necessarily translate into barriers against countries and, if it must, then for how long? In October 2002, the President of the EU Commission, Romano Prodi, spoke for the first time about *a priori* geographical limits to EU expansion. The good news is that, despite his position, Mr Prodi has no authority to speak for the EU on this matter, and his position plainly contradicts that set out in the EU's principal (and founding) documents. What is more, later EU summits produced a far more encouraging message.

The bad news is that "dividing lines" are being drawn *de facto* by the differences in political, security, and business culture already discussed. Worse, the policies of the EU—notably the Schengen accords and the Common Agricultural Policy—are strengthening these divisions and, what is more, adding some new and highly arbitrary ones. Few could claim that internal conditions in Albania and Bosnia-Herzegovina warrant a status for these countries superior to that afforded Moldova or Ukraine, yet in some respects they enjoy such a status. Few could claim that these discrepancies strengthen the "European impulse" in, let alone the security of, Moldova or Ukraine. But the EU needs to ask a more radical question. Will its policy towards these eastern neighbors strengthen the influence or the security of the EU itself? There are three reasons to doubt this.

First, the EU Schengen border has the potential to create a false sense of security. The lesser but still very serious problem will be posed by the contradictory and often harmful regimes on the remaining borders of EU neighbor states. Moldova's border with Ukraine and Ukraine's border with Russia are salient, but not exclusive examples. Up until 2003, Russia's official position has been that the Ukraine-Russia border should be delimited (drawn on maps) but not demarcated.[2] If it is true (as alleged by the State Committee on the State Border of Ukraine) that this border is the point of entry for two-thirds of contraband and 90 per cent of illegal migrants into the country, Russian border policy not only places a huge burden on Ukraine; it is likely to put strains upon the Schengen system as well. Obviously, the elimination of Schengen would not diminish this problem.

But the Schengen system creates the illusion, echoed in EU policy, that the eastern border of Ukraine is a bilateral issue rather than an issue for Europe. This leads to the greater problem. For if neighbouring states perceive that the EU regards their vulnerabilities and pressures as somebody else's business, that business will certainly grow and the spectre of the EU's future neighbors as sources of "additional threats to European countries in terms of drugs, weapons,

2. The standard principle was reiterated by the Russian Federation Foreign Ministry on 16 August 2001, when it stated that 'the Russian-Ukrainian border should be a border of peace, accord and interaction; it should unite not separate the people of our countries . . . The formation of artificial barriers and obstacles would contradict these objectives and complicate contacts between people and cooperation between economic entities, especially in frontier areas.' (Interfax, *BBC Summary of World Broadcasts* 16 August 2001.)

illegal immigrants, prostitutes and ecological disasters" (and, one might add, money laundering and terrorism) could become a reality.[3] In sum, the Schengen system, seen as a "new iron curtain" in much of Eastern Europe, could become Europe's new Maginot line instead.

Second, the EU's detached and reactive approach to negative developments in neighboring states ignores the powerful connection between its own policies and these very developments. Dated, protectionist mechanisms (notably the Common Agricultural Policy) deprive the Union of the greatest lever it possesses to encourage transformation in neighbouring countries: trade. Adherence to these mechanisms also undermines the Union's moral authority and puts in a cynical light the demand that *others* reform. In post-Communist countries, "reform" is not a set of technical and administrative challenges. It is a political undertaking that can only advance by challenging relations of power. In these countries, those called upon to mount these challenges are being asked to risk their careers, livelihoods, and, in some cases, their own safety. They will not entertain these risks without the moral conviction that their efforts are valued, supported, and joined by more powerful partners. This requires the EU to present a hard-headed, conditional, but clear perspective of EU membership over the long term. By declining to offer such a perspective to neighbors, the EU signals that whatever the latter do to solve their problems, the "greater Europe" will be built without them. For this reason, it demoralizes its natural supporters and swells the ranks of those who believe that meaningful change is not possible. Until it re-examines its own policy, the EU will not only fail to broaden its constituency in these states, it will weaken the constituency it has.

Third and consequently, EU policy not only fortifies the impression that the Union is a closed bloc. It gives credibility to efforts to create an alternative. The Eurasian Economic Union (*EvrAzES*), relaunched as the Eurasian Economic Zone, is testimony to the vigor and effectiveness of President Putin's integrationist policy, as well as his success in diminishing "multi-voicedness" (*mnogogolosiye*) in the Russian Federation itself. Within several CIS

3. Anatoliy Grytsenko, *Civil-Military Relations in Ukraine: A System Emerging from Chaos* (Groningen, Netherlands: Centre for European Security Studies, Harmonie Paper 1, 1997), p. 1.

countries, the enterprise is also in step with the thinking and interests of several national elites, and it has a definite economic logic. But for better or worse, its logic is contrary to that of the enlarging European Union, where norms of business are not only different from, but largely incompatible with the trans-national business culture dominant in "former Soviet space."

Today many claim that President Putin understands that this business culture is an obstacle to Russia's integration with Europe. That might well be so. But Putin has consistently relied upon this business culture in his efforts to create "a good-neighborly belt along the perimeter of Russia's borders,"[4] and for the most part his business partners in Belarus, Ukraine, and Moldova come from the ranks of those who have obstructed the introduction of EU standards of transparency, openness, law, and contract enforcement in their own countries. In several CIS countries, these integrationist efforts have been a source of tension, and they could prove to be a source of instability.

## CONCLUSION

Foreign policy and international relations definitely aggravate the soft security challenges besetting Central and Eastern Europe, and changes in these policies can definitely improve them. But the reflexive response to these problems, "strengthening international mechanisms," is largely irrelevant to their causes, dynamics, or solutions. Today there is an abundance of such mechanisms, perhaps a super-abundance of them, yet the underlying problems are not improving. The fundamental source of these problems lies in internal policies and the internal condition of states. International integration will not succeed until governments become legitimate in the eyes of their own people, countries become integrated within themselves, and states develop in compatible directions.

Where soft security is concerned, the future will depend less on the nature of ties between Moscow and Brussels or even Moscow and Kiev than between Moscow and Makhachkala, Lviv and Donetsk,

4. This is the objective defined in Russia's *Concepts of Foreign Policy*, approved by President Putin on 28 June 2000.

Chisinau and Tiraspol. Today Western European and Russian policy, on the one hand, and East-Central European practice on the other, are dividing Europe. If we continue to take refuge in mechanisms and avoid political struggle and urgent practical steps, this process will continue, and we will merely confirm the homespun American truth: "Keep doing what you're doing, and you'll keep getting what you've got."

# MANAGING SOFT SECURITY THREATS: CURRENT PROGRESS AND FUTURE PROSPECTS

ANNE ALDIS AND GRAEME HERD

## RECONCEPTUALIZING SECURITY IN THE POST-COLD WAR WORLD

The collapse of the Cold War order highlighted shortfalls in the existing and accepted analytical and conceptual frameworks constructed to provide us with mental maps to more easily comprehend the nature of inter-state power relations. If it can be said that most

We would like to thank and acknowledge the effort of Jone Gittinger, who on behalf of the Conference Center, George C. Marshall European Center for Security Studies, organized the 'Managing the Challenges of Soft Security Threats in the Twenty First Century Conference,' April 7–9, 2004 in Garmisch-Partenkirchen, Germany. This conference provided the inspiration for this edited special issue of 'European Security.'

concepts in the social sciences are contested, then none more so than the scope and nature of "security." What are the causes of insecurity and what policies are best able to lessen the impact of these threats to societies, states, regions, and the global international system?

Despite its contested nature, most analysts agree that it is "the threat to use, or the actual use of, force that essentially demarcates the study and practice of security as a discipline distinct from the broader study and practice of international relations."[1]

Yet within the threat of force can be contained other forms of pressure, and as a consequence of the changes in the global balance of power after the end of the Cold War two predominant views of security had an influence on policy-makers. One argued for a "narrow" definition of security while the other favored a "wider" agenda. As the decade progressed the wide or "extended" definition was generally accepted as providing the most useful framework through which to understand insecurity in the transformed international system.

"Narrowers" focus on the military aspects of security and have argued that the key element of strategic analysis is the possible use of force. They concede that non-military elements of security may occupy more of the strategist's attention than previously, but, ultimately, military security should remain the primary focus of analysis as this security sector continued to pose the greatest and most profound and far-reaching threats to states.

Security was still to be fundamentally understood as based upon the state, and particularly on the necessity of states to fulfil their raison d'être—survival. Security for them concerned the study of the threat, and use and control of military force. Yet even they accepted that national security could no longer be construed in simple Cold War terms—as cognate with "defense" in which the concepts of deterrence and containment would prevent an invasion by the West or the East, depending on one's perspective in Washington, DC or Moscow.

The "wideners" questioned the primacy of the military element of the security debate. They argued that the focus on territorial

---

1. Terrif, Terry, 'Environmental Degradation and Security', in Richard H. Shultz, Jr., Roy Godson, and George H. Quester, *Security Studies for the 21st Century* (Washington, DC and London, Brassey's Publications Ltd., 1997), p. 253.

integrity of the state and traditional conceptions of sovereignty in which security encompassed the stability of the core institutions of the state and the integrity of state decision-making structures, ought to be widened to include societal (and human), economic, and environmental security. Thus, security was perceived to mean more than simple military might and publics and elites alike understood and measured it increasingly in terms of the impact and scope of non-military threats on the daily lives of peoples and the integrity of states. These threats included corruption; criminal groups; private militias; insecure borders; smuggling and trafficking in weapons, drugs, contraband and people; illegal migration; proliferation of nuclear, chemical, and biological weapons of mass destruction (WMD); environmental scarcity (for example, access to fresh water or cropland), and, of course, terrorism.

"Economic security," for example, became a particular focus of interest following the collapse of the Russian, South American, and South East Asian economies in 1998, as the social, political, and economic fabric and even government stability of these states was threatened by currency speculation and the structural inflexibility of their economies. For some states the rapid growth of criminal influence upon governance has undermined the moral authority and legitimacy of the state, as national and local power structures are "colonized" by criminal groups. The very nature of criminal activities—particularly the financial ones of tax evasion, money laundering, and embezzlement of state funds—all weaken the resources of the state, thereby limiting its ability to fulfil its federal functions and administrative capacity at a local level. Criminal activities also distort the working of a market economy and the international standing of the state, so threatening its political and economic integration with the rest of the world. Political elites that act in criminal ways subvert democratic norms, corrupt legislatures, and undermine civil society.

In some cases "failed states" emerge, that is, states that are considered 'failed' because they are "incapable of projecting power and asserting authority within their own borders."[2] Haiti in the Caribbean,

2. Rotberg, Robert I., 'Failed States in a World of Terror', *Foreign Affairs*, Vol. 81, Issue 4, (2002), p. 128.

Sudan in Africa, and Afghanistan in Central Asia serve as examples from three continents of failed states. They were characterized by the prevalence of famines, ethnic, tribal, religious, and other sectional or communal conflicts and dislocations, which undermine, destabilize, or otherwise challenge the political authority and stability of the state. Conflict can be exacerbated by the presence of oppressive rulers/dictators who despoil and weaken their own states and threaten others—President Idi Amin in Uganda in the 1970s, or President Saddam Hussein of Iraq until April 2003 provide such examples. State recovery is challenged by a weakened state capacity, deeply divided societies, devastated economies, squandered resources, and traumatized populations.

As these political elites tend to have access to military force, and so hold a monopoly of power within a contested territory, they present complex challenges and "credibility traps" for foreign intervention. In these states or quasi-states combatant and non-combatant roles are difficult to distinguish, army, paramilitary, and armed group status cannot easily be separated out, and it is in the interest of local power elites—criminal warlords—to maintain the instability and institutionalize the status quo. The tri-border area between Argentina, Brazil, and Paraguay constitutes one such lawless region in South America; Eritrea, Somalia, and Sudan in East Africa another.

The break-up of large multiethnic states in the early 1990s (in particular, Yugoslavia and the Soviet Union) raised the prospect that such states are unsustainable in the contemporary international global system. It suggested that the 21st century might be characterized by the collapse of others (India, China, Indonesia, Nigeria, and Brazil are possible contenders; surprisingly, the world's largest multiethnic state, the US, is not on the list—this suggests that their fragility must be ascribed to other causes than ethnicity).

Certainly, in some cases state break-up is associated with "ethnic cleansing" and ethno-nationalist state building projects. These tendencies have increased interest in "societal security." Societal security focuses on the integrity of societal identity and the various factors that can undermine that integrity, destabilize a state or communities, and precipitate a series of violence outcomes. As a result, inter-communal violence, civil war, and inter-state conflict became a higher priority object of attention for analysts and security policy-makers and practitioners. This is reflected in the growing sophistication of conflict prevention tools, crisis management policies, and post-conflict reconstruction or rehabilitation programs, applied, for example, with varying degrees of success, to Bosnia-Herzegovina in 1995 and onwards, East Timor after 1999, Afghanistan after 2001, and Iraq in 2003.

While some analysts accepted that the traditional military-security definition should be expanded to include economic and societal security concerns, environmental security was for many a bridge too far. It is undeniable that as two-thirds of the world's population live in areas with a quarter of the world's fresh rainfall, fresh water supplies, particularly ground water, are under increasing strain. If global warming changes in rainfall patterns and rising sea levels continue then the Gangetic plain off North India and Bangladesh would become threatened—and with it 500 million and their communities.

However, the causal relationship between the environment and conflict is more contested, though it has been demonstrated in a variety of ways. They noted that "environmental scarcity" could be characterized by the lack of land, water or timber, for example. This scarcity contributed to societal stress, political instability, and economic hardship. The migration of rural communities to urban slums, where high unemployment, widespread poverty, and poor education were prevalent, provided the social base for charismatic leaders with liberation ideologies and dynamic organizations to capitalize on community disintegration, group radicalization, and social explosions. These groups were particularly powerful when—as in Mexico—one exclusive ethnic or social group controlled access to key resources to the disadvantage of another group.

Competition for environmental resources themselves might become a cause of conflict, as opposing factions fought to obtain or retain control over them. The wars in Central (the Democratic Republic of Congo), West (Sierra Leone) and South West (Angola) Africa have been fought for the control of mineral resources (in particular "blood diamonds" and precious metals) and timber. These commodities have funded the conflict and it is the promise of great wealth that has sustained these forgotten wars in Africa. Access to water supplies has frequently been posited as a future source of conflict in Africa, the Middle East, and Central Asia.

Whatever the cause of the conflict, the "CNN factor" ensures that there will always be calls for international intervention. Some of these calls might even be heeded, and the international community's primary response tool tends to be a military one, only later followed by aid packages for the economy and civil society building. The devastation of the environment itself or environmental infrastructure might also become a war aim—a means of inflicting unacceptable pain upon an enemy state or people in order to prevail in conflict. It might also constitute the means to inflict a Parthian blow in defeat, as was the case with Saddam Hussein setting fire to the oil fields in Kuwait in 1991 when his invasion was repulsed. There is thus a clear continuum between hard and soft security problems, responses, and solutions.

Although the environment-conflict nexus is of rising strategic importance for states and international organizations, in many cases the effects of conflict upon the environment are unintentional and the impact usually international rather than national, demanding non-military responses to manage the disaster or catastrophe. Whilst it can be argued that environmental factors are much more likely to act as an increased incentive for international and regional co-operation, the evidence for such a contention is questionable. Although the proposals for inter-state environmental cooperation are plentiful—for example, the international Jordan Valley Water Authority (linking Israel, Jordan, Syria, and Palestine) has discussed the potential for managing water sharing for the last 40 years whilst similar projects are proposed in Central Asia to halt the shrinkage and pollution of the Aral Sea—little practical cooperation is forthcoming.

However, faced with a real threat to public health, the non-military responses can be encouraging. The January 2004 outbreak of avian flu and that of SARS in March 2003, spreading rapidly from Beijing to Hong Kong, Singapore, Tokyo, and Toronto, highlighted the difficulties of coordinating effective responses by international and national actors. Whilst a biological weapon did not cause the epidemic, the swift and effective international responses to it showed a useful learning curve, and may have deterred future biological WMD attacks.

## SOFT SECURITY PARADIGMS AND THE POST-POST COLD WAR ERA?

With the fall of the Berlin Wall in 1989 and the euphoria that accompanied the end of the Cold War, the expectation among most scholars, analysts, and practitioners was two-fold. First, that the newly emergent—in some cases restored—independent states would in the post-Cold War era move from authoritarian state-building towards democratizing their political systems, economies, and foreign and security policies. As a result the international system would be characterized by the gradual proliferation of a zone of peace and stability as the threat of armed conflict, use of force, military power, and nuclear devastation declined and, ultimately, disappeared.

Francis Fukuyama was the first to suggest that 1989 represented the triumph of market capitalism and liberal democratic ideology over all possible alternatives. The ideological dialectic that had shaped the international system had been reduced after 1945 to competition between capitalism and communism. In the post-Cold War world, "market-democracy" was set to become the modernization project of choice for all states. The future of the international system was to be characterised by the gradual democratization and consolidation of market-democratic institutions, policies, values, and culture. Liberal institutionalism—internationally generated norms, procedures and institutions for the enforcement of mutually agreed legal frameworks—would, ultimately, lead to the replacement of international anarchy with the international rule of law.

The adherents of democratization predicted that as a result, tensions and cleavages within and between the states would gradually diminish, as all integrated into a globalized economy. Democratic states shared the same norms and values and as a result enjoyed the efficiency of inter-democratic bargaining and conflict resolution. It was also argued that democratic states choose their wars more wisely than non-democratic states, have larger economies, form stronger alliances, and make better and more consensual decisions. The soft security threats that were beginning to be conceptualized in theoretical discourse would be shared by all states, and the developed world could put its peace dividend to good use in overcoming them on a global scale.

By 1993 Samuel Huntington, analyzing the same events as Fukuyama, offered a radically divergent interpretation.[3] Huntington

3. Fukuyama, Francis, 'The End of History?', *The National Interest*, Summer 1989, pp. 3–18; Huntington, Samuel., *The Clash of Civilizations and the Remaking of the World Order* (Norman Okla: University of Oklahoma Press, 1996).

argued that as a consequence of the breakdown of the Cold War order, the future was not one of "democratic peace" and cooperation within a single global system in which the triumph of Western-style modernity was set to create one universal world civilization, but rather continual and protracted wars between "civilisational blocs."

Seven civilizations spanned the globe, each characterized by a belief system and the values it encapsulated. Western Christianity, Slavic Orthodoxy, Islam, Buddhism, Hinduism, Confucianism and "possibly African" civilizations were now unconstrained by rigid bipolar stability. Although the Soviet Union had been a superpower with foreign and security policy objectives that were global in reach, with the collapse of the Soviet bloc Russia had been downgraded to a major power. It had regional security interests—particularly in the former Soviet Central Asia and the South Caucasus—and a civilizational resonance as the core state of Slavic Orthodoxy. Where civilizations brushed up against each other, Huntington noted, cultural fault-lines could be identified and it was along these fault-lines that future conflicts were most likely to occur. This left hanging the question of where the cultural fault lines were in the Caucasus and Central Asia—was Ukraine to be divided? These quibbles aside, a "Clash of Civilizations" paradigm emerged to challenge that of the "End of History."

Both of these mutually exclusive paradigms have been subjected to powerful attack, although they are not entirely discounted. Neither of them was considered a sufficient explanation to account for the myriad changes and new security threats that dominate the international system. In particular, some that focused on the impact of globalization argue that Huntington and Fukuyama failed to appreciate the extent to which a fast changing globalization challenges the ability of a state to drive forward the process of state modernization. Improvements in technology, communications, and transport increased inter-connectedness among peoples, societies, states, and regions, underpinning the idea of a "global village." By the mid- to late-1990s globalization was increasingly promoted as a process that offered to account for integratory pressures and fragmentation processes ("fragmegration") unleashed by ever-closer global interconnectedness. It was noted that there appeared greater disparities in per capita income, the share of world trade and foreign direct investment among North America, the EU, and the Asian Tiger economies (the triad states) with their open economies and the rest of the world. Is the globalization process a constructive force for peace and stability or an unintentional dynamic for destruction and conflict?[4]

Increasingly, critiques of international capitalism—which was perceived by many as the cutting edge of the globalization process—argued that it was a force for oppression, exploitation, and injustice, undermining traditional cultures and communities and increasing income inequalities within and between states leading to political disintegration, the growth of failed states, and, ultimately, the promotion of stateless, decentralized criminal and terrorist networks. "Exclusive globalization," it was argued, was the reality, rather than an "inclusive globalization" process. The exclusive nature of globalization supported the closely interdependent triad states, exacerbating divisions between "winners" and non-industrializing "losers" in the globalization process.

This outcome—the creation of "20/80" societies in which elites benefited at the expense of the majority of the world's population, was a source of conflict. In short, the markets, multinationals, the IMF, World Bank, and World Trade Organization—the institutional embodiment of globalization—undermined the role and function of the state (sovereignty and territorial integrity) and, indeed, democracy. The violent anti-globalist movements from Seattle (2000) through to Milan (2001) appeared as the radical forefront of a transnational under-current of unease at the perceived destructiveness of globalization.

However, others that have studied the impact of globalization upon security and stability have understood globalization as a dual process, with some states benefiting from "thick globalization" and its attendant sources of stability, others from "thin globalization" and the insecurities that follow. Here it is argued that the "functioning core" of the globalized world embodies rule sets, norms, and ties that bind it in mutually assured dependence. This thick globalization is characterized by network connectivity, financial transactions, liberal media flows, and collective security systems that

4. Hoffman, Stanley, 'Clash of Globalizations', *Foreign Affairs*, Vol. 81, No. 4, July/August 2002, pp. 104–115.

underpin stable governments and populations enjoying rising living standards. Open economies lead to interdependence and greater prosperity and decrease the likelihood of insecurity. These states perform well according to the standard indicators—per capita GDP, UN "Human Development Index," Transparency International's "Corruption Perception Index," and Freedom House's 'Freedom in the World' report.

By contrast, thin globalization allows politically repressive regimes to consolidate, which can be characterized in extreme cases by the prevalence of widespread poverty, corruption, high infant mortality, disease, disenfranchisement, marginalization, and massacres. These regions have been called the "non-integrating gap"—they cannot control their borders, they suffer from ethnic and religious conflict and export insecurity—and they constitute a strategic threat environment for the functioning core. Indeed, as four-fifths of the world's oil reserves lie within this non-integrating gap, the potential for resource wars is high. Seam states, such as Greece, Mexico, Brazil, Indonesia, and Pakistan, lie between the non-integrating gap and the functioning core.

Tajikistan in Central Asia and Lebanon in the Eastern Mediterranean demonstrate the ability of some states to gradually recover from near collapse, while East Timor in South East Asia and Bosnia-Herzegovina and Kosovo in the Balkans also illustrate the ability of the international community to effectively organize protectorates and trusteeships to stabilise troubled and turbulent regions. The extent that both the international community and these seam states are able to play a major role in containing the spill over of insecurity into the functioning core and then roll back the non-integrating gap will largely shape security politics in the 21st century. Many of the challenges they face are soft—trafficking in people and drugs, corruption, environmental degradation through deforestation, and other agricultural practices. Much international effort is being devoted to trying to eliminate them, with the recognition that such problems managed at source contribute to the security of other countries too. However, the consolidation of such efforts is complicated by the dynamic impact of September 11, 2001 (9/11), on the divergent security priorities, policies, and strategies that many states have subsequently adopted.

In the early 21st century and hard on the heels of the events of 9/11, many analysts argued that international politics had been irrevocably transformed. One view was that a new paradigm had replaced those of the 1990s—a US-led "global war on terror" (GWOT)—in which, as President Bush argued, democratic and other "freedom-loving" states struggle against an "axis of evil" (Iran, Iraq, North Korea), and global terror networks and transnational terrorist groups, such as *al-Qa'idah.* This war was to target terrorist groups that were global in scope and was projected to last decades rather than the term of a single administration. Terrorism had now publicly blurred the dividing line between internal and external security, and state responses included the integration of diplomatic, economic, military, and intelligence responses to prevent terrorist attacks, reduce state and societies' vulnerabilities to such attacks, minimize the impact of such attacks when they did occur, and recover quickly from such attacks ('resilience').

## RECONSIDERING SOFT SECURITY IN LIGHT OF THE POST-9/11 PARADIGM

In the Cold War the US had built coalitions to contain communism and protect the "free world," making it safe for democracy and capitalism. In the new century, it appears that the US and its allies are rebuilding "coalitions of the willing" to protect market-democratic states and contain global terror. The shocking impact of 9/11 determined that the Bush administration "would seek to dominate the international system to such an extent that no strategic challenge would ever again be posed." While the US has a huge weapons and technology advantage over its nearest rivals, does this power allow the US to set the international security agenda, or, indeed, force it to provide security for all in the new century? Should military weapons in all instances be preferred to those that build soft security, and by doing so build states' capacity to manage the combined threats of terrorism and other forms of criminality? One of the goals of the US strategy for combating international terrorism is to reduce its scope and capacity to inflict massive destruction, to the extent that it is "recriminalised" and can be dealt with by domestic law enforcement means.[5] Here again is evidence of the continuum between hard and soft security.

Despite the much-hyped "translatlantic rift" exposed by the intervention in Iraq, there are two constant threads that run through the Euro-Atlantic security tapestry. First, at the fundamental level, the US and European states are based on liberal political cultures and have common interests and goals (global justice, democratization, stability) and a shared security community, if not strategic culture. However, there has been a growing divergence within and between members of the Euro-Atlantic security community over the means by which these shared ends were to be achieved. One key disagreement has emerged over what justifies coercive intervention and how, where, and when to use force. NATO allies tended to agree on what the threats were, but disagreed as to their priority, characteristics and the most appropriate methods and instruments to deploy when responding to these threats. Such divergence in the means (not ends) to achieve security and stability has shaped debates concerning the likely future transformation of NATO: containing communism brought unity of purpose; containing terrorism has not.

Second, US hard military power will remain an Olympian constant—with the military emulating the self-same ethos (longer, faster, higher). But is the US now at the apex of its power—unable to resist the temptation to climb even higher? Some might argue that the logic of the US strategy is to create a de facto global, albeit liberal, democratic empire, through the creation of trusteeships and neo-colonial protectorates that were formerly failed states (where local tyrants and terrorists flourished), and that such an ambitious program will necessitate the acceptance of the need to act in concert with other states.[6] Thus the US will become more dependent on informal, multilateral institutions and ad hoc coalitions and groupings, rather than formalized, institutionalised, rules-based alliances, to assure the global security it seeks.

---

5. Michael Mihalka, presentation at conference 'Countering Terrorism: Strategies and Concepts', sponsored by the George C. Marshall Center, Conflict Studies Research Centre and Institute of World Economy and International Relations, Garmisch-Partenkirchen, 1–3 December 2003.

6. Cooper, Robert, *The Breaking of Nations: Order and Chaos in the Twenty-First Century* (London: Atlantic, 2003).

As Julian Lindley-French argues, in general, the post-Cold War era has been characterized by a blurring of boundaries between hard and soft, civil and military, leading to what he has termed a revolution in security affairs. According to his "hard America/soft Europe" thesis, the EU adopts a soft security agenda as a cloak for "strategic pretense"—a fundamental inability to deploy coercive power alongside the US.[7]

Thus, 9/11 and the "battle for Afghanistan" and the "battle for Iraq" have highlighted structural, technological, and institutional weaknesses and tensions within the transatlantic security community—the birthplace of the modern Westphalian state system. It has also caused a reaction around the globe as many states struggle to respond to the new security environment at the start of a century which, it appears, will be dominated by a paradoxical force – a US-led liberal democratic imperial project which will impose democratic values in place of terrorists and tyrants.

However, rather than representing a terrible new future—atrocious as the events in New York and Washington, DC were—9/11 can best be understood as bringing into sharper focus the nature and pace of security and conflict-related developments in the decade since the end of the Cold War. These changes are numerous and interlinked, but three processes are particularly notable, and pose difficult challenges to the stability of states—even the most wealthy, well-organized, and powerful - and the international system.[8]

First, changes in the global balance of power brought about by the end of the Soviet Union and the growing gap between rich and poor countries still have to be properly understood and dealt with by policy-makers. Second, the technological revolution poses threats to all states—the weak and the powerful. Third, the changing public attitude—particularly notable in Western societies—to the role, mission, and duties of the military is occurring at a time when new sources of insecurity are becoming more numerous and profound. Collectively, while these processes have made the study of security extremely interesting, they have also rendered the security

7. Lyndley-French, Julian 'In the Shade of Locarno? Why European Defence is Failing', *International Affairs*, 78, 4 (2002), pp. 789–811.
8. Carothers, Thomas 'Promoting Democracy and Fighting Terror', *Foreign Affairs*, Vol. 82, No. 1, January/February 2003, pp. 84–97.

challenges, obstacles, and dilemmas for states and regions alike much harder to conceptualize and overcome. Thus, while the Westphalia state model remains a primary guide—sovereignty, boundaries, armed forces, national interest—in the world today, many states lack the capacity to live up to the model.[9] No state, even the US, can state categorically that it can protect itself and its interests absolutely against the primary threats in today's world.

Hard security in which military force ("hard power") was deployed by militaries against combatants for territorial gains or defence is increasingly perceived to be superseded by soft security—non-military threats that could be managed through recourse to the military, but more appropriately non-military instruments, such as diplomatic, economic, financial, and intelligence strategies or policies, instruments which formed the mainstay of "soft power." Lindley-French's introduction to this volume highlights the threat continuum among transnational organized crime, catastrophic terror, corrupt regimes in some weak states, and the fact that "[A]ny response therefore requires holistic, strategic, pan-national civil-military responses working within states and between states, often with a global reach."

Both hard and soft power—the hard and soft security approaches—must be coordinated in order to defeat terrorist threats, but it is primarily soft power that can be most effectively deployed to manage the variety of soft security threats, only a few of which this volume has addressed. These are the tools that Europe has chosen to emphasize in the war on terrorism too, but it is clear from David Brown's analysis in this volume that more must be done to make the European border control instruments into an effective strategy for improving Europe's soft security situation as a whole.

## CONSPECTUS

The concept of security can therefore be seen to reflect the concerns of particular states in specific periods. Security is a particularly malleable and flexible concept and a study of security politics reveals as much about the objective nature of stability and

9. Krauthammer, Charles, 'The Unipolar Moment Revisited', *The National Interest*, No. 70, Winter 2002/2003, pp. 5–20.

instability as about the subjective perceptions of the societies and states that use it.

Looking to the future, how might demographic and environmental change, science and technology, globalization, national and international governance, and future conflict affect the security of individuals, societies, states, regions, and the global international system? Although the evolution and impact of these key global trends and dynamics are difficult for the student of international relations to discern, the questions themselves are of importance. Our study of these issues will allow us to anticipate and hopefully better manage future sources of insecurity and conflict and so gradually manage the proliferation of sustainable peace globally.

In reviewing the articles gathered in this volume, it is clear that the nature of the threat shapes the extent to which it can be alleviated and the perceptions of the relative prominence of these threats shapes also the types of instruments states can deploy to manage them. It is also clear that both of the issues addressed here—illegal migration and trafficking—straddle the continuum between hard and soft security concerns, and therefore can be useful case studies in pinpointing future directions both for academic discourse and for policy formulation. As Ryabikhin and Viktorova argue in their paper: "The weapons black market is highly criminalised, with strong linkages between arms and human trafficking and the illicit narcotics trade, which all fuel various types of low intensity conflict." All our authors agree that criminal networks appear highly adaptable, sophisticated, well-equipped, effective, and willing to cooperate with each other, and treat all trafficking and smuggling activities as a single type of transaction, moving whatever commodity is most in demand, and along their standard route networks.

Leonid Polyakov and Irina Ivakhniouk examine the issue of illegal migration, and both articles illustrate the nature of the threat continuum. Irina Ivakhniouk highlights the role that states play in this process, arguing that they constitute key links in a Euro-Asian "migration system," comprising often-willing donor and receiver countries.

And yet illegal migration is identified as a national security threat. This is because, in the words of Polyakov, illegal migration drains "the human and financial resources of the state, contributes to a high level of criminality and corruption, and negatively impacts on the international image of the country."

Ivakhniouk argues that in Russia: "The negative degree of these effects is maybe even higher because illegal migrants disorganise a national labour market that is on the path to market economy; they increase illegal employment niches and, consequently, impede the transition process."

However, she also notes that with a 30% labor shortfall in 2002, Russia needs migrants and the question for the state is whether they are to be legal or illegal. This dilemma has recently also been faced by the UK, which has eventually responded to its illegal migrant crisis of the 1990s by making legal migration much easier.

Illegal migration can thus have detrimental effects on all countries involved in the continuum. Migration often acts as a pressure valve for donor countries that are suffering social tensions. Yet the illegal nature of the migration restricts its potential to act as a normal process, allowing the return of the migrant with enhanced skills, as well as complicating his remittance of earnings to prop up the societal security of his home country. Transit countries suffer, not least because of the perception of ineffective government, because of lax or inadequate border controls. Recipient countries suffer too, because of the distortion of their economies by the burgeoning black and grey sectors.

Lest this might portray illegal migration as a relatively benign activity from which only the impersonal state suffers, it must be emphasised that the criminal groups who organize the activity exhibit callous disregard for the welfare of their "commodity" in transit—deaths are not infrequent—and the exorbitant fees charged for what are often unsuccessful and repeated attempts impose severe social strains and distort local economies to a significant extent. Illegal migration is only the most palatable of the trafficking activities all along the chain of supply and demand.

Most commonly, the female and child migrants are forced, lured, or deceived into prostitution or volunteer for it out of desperation. In the recipient countries, the prevalence of such activities, even if conducted legally, characterizes a society in need of a safety valve; it is not an honorable transaction characteristic of a secure, thriving, equitable democracy. Much more worthy of contumely is the trade in human organs, prolonging the lives of the rich at the expense of those of the poor. Even those who are reluctant to accept the concept of societal security must concede that none of these activities are tokens of a healthy society, and that they must be addressed by the developed world as indigenous problems, not simply as the aspirations and desperations of those in poorer countries exported to their doors.

It therefore follows that the plethora of mechanisms and border control regimes outlined by several contributors to this volume will never, however effectively they are used, be sufficient to halt the traffic. To focus on these as the most effective means of ensuring soft security, by analogy with military capabilities in ensuring hard security, reveals a fundamental misunderstanding of the nature of the threats to a state's stability. While they can be an effective means of strengthening what Pratt's article in this volume calls a "culture of lawfulness" the types of threats they help to contain are not susceptible to the same kind of "deter and destroy" strategy that characterises military security. These are threats that must be managed and reduced to an acceptable level, rather than eliminated altogether.

Soft security threats pose risks to ethics and quality of life as well as to the economic well-being and hence to a state's ability to function. Soft security threats can prove just as damaging to a state's capacity to act, to its capacity to make strategic decisions and thus to its ability to govern. These threats are just as real as are those posed by harder, more normally defined military threats to the stability and therefore security of a state. State strategies, both internally and globally, should therefore concentrate on defining an acceptable level of risk, managing it effectively, and working towards its future reduction. The reason for doing so hardly requires further elucidation, but the means are worthy of more serious study: those outlined in the present volume, against only a few of these threats, hardly inspire confidence. Yet there is no space here to enlarge on this subject. We can, however, touch briefly on where and how the crossover between hard and soft security can occur, and thus offer a pointer towards future, more effective action.

The hard edges of the soft security threat can most easily be seen in the weakest of the states that have emerged in the Balkans, Eastern Europe, and the Caucasus over the last decade. Here, ineffective governments in territories awash with weapons are hostages to those with vested interests in criminal activity. Here, too, can be seen the effects of societal and environmental degradation. Whatever the merits of the separatists' claims in Transdneistria and Abkhazia, to name but two, there can be little doubt that the territories they control provide a safe haven for illegal transfers of money, weapons and other commodities. It is also widely believed that terrorist networks, operating on a global scale, seek out and benefit from these safe havens and illicit trade networks. True, they plan, procure, and operate also in strong states such as the US and UK. But there it is much more difficult for the networks to escape detection. In both (albeit by deception in the West) they can take advantage of the state's desire to derive economic benefit from its financial markets and weapons industry.

This brings us back to globalization, with all its benefits and pitfalls. If one accepts the world as a single global marketplace for goods and services, the traffic will naturally tend to converge towards localities where people can afford to buy, and where migrants believe they can benefit most from what they have to offer. Hence, routes for commodities and people tend to drive westwards, where the opportunities are greater than at home. If the imbalance between "home" and "away" economies was lessened, and the profit margin on the drugs trade made less advantageous, much of the illegal traffic might in time be eliminated. This simplistic argument is not offered as a panacea. It certainly will not eliminate the criminal networks, which will simply seek other means of making money. But it does encapsulate two characteristics which soft security shares with hard military security: first, that problems have more chance of being managed successfully if tackled at a global level, and, second, that there is no such thing as a zero sum game in either hard or soft security.

# INDEX